MW01257442

"Wisdom That Transforms. Action That Lasts."

Our Commitment

We believe that true wisdom has the power to transform lives. Our mission is to equip readers with timeless insights and practical tools that inspire growth, guide decisions, and empower purposeful living. We don't just inform—we empower.

Our books combine profound understanding with real-life application, enabling readers to unlock their potential and navigate life's challenges with clarity and confidence. With each step guided by wisdom, we help you create lasting change and live the life you deserve.

When wisdom meets purpose, transformation follows.

Copyright

ISBN   978-1-952359-43-9   (paperback)
ISBN   978-1-952359-44-6   (ebook)
Audiobook Available   (Amazon.com and Audible.com)

"Practical Wisdom for Real-Life Challenges!

For More Information About the Life Planning Series:

www.lifeplanningtools.com

**Life Planning Series
by J. S. Wellman**

CHOOSE A
Positive
Self-Image

Self-Identity, Self-Esteem,
and Self-Worth

J. S. Wellman

LIFE PLANNING SERIES
J.S. WELLMAN

Extra-mile Publishing

Table of Contents

Message From the Author

Unlock Your Potential with Timeless Wisdom!

The general purpose of this book and the Life Planning Series is to encourage you to pursue actions and character traits that will produce your best life. The Series addresses ten different activities or traits that help people improve their lives, and *CHOOSE Core Values* addresses sixteen separate core values that you might consider beneficial.

Understand that you can improve or acquire high personal character and outstanding habits, no matter how good or bad your life may be at the moment. Good personal character and life habits can be achieved.

You don't have to read all the books in this series to make a significant change or improvement in your life. Find the books that focus on the areas of your life that you want to improve and dig in.

Know that this is a progressive journey. You don't need to climb the highest mountain immediately. You may just want to learn more about the basic principles and concepts. This Series and this book will provide you with a foundation for decisions relative to your lifestyle, goals, priorities, and commitments.

The key to developing high character and making good decisions in your life is *intentionality*. The Life Planning Series will help you identify the path you want to travel but you will need to be intentional about walking that path. If you want to make progress toward the goal of living a better life, you must intentionally take action.

Change will require making good decisions, establishing important core values in your life, setting priorities, and making commitments. This book will help you identify the values in life that will produce your goals and objectives. High personal character and good habits can be achieved if you want them.

This Series is designed to help you smooth out the path for your life journey. But, remember, all actions (both words and deeds) have consequences. These consequences will impact you and all those around you.

The key to your success is: "*Decide you want to do it and work at it regularly.*"

Steve

"*Set your mind on your future and commit to being the very best you can be!*"
Stephen H Berkey[2]

"Wisdom to decide and the steps to succeed."

Free PDF

Wise Decision-Making
[Get the ebook version for 99 cents]

We want to give you a <u>free</u> copy of:

Wise Decision-Making:
You can make good choices.

This book will help you make good
decisions in your life, career, family . . .

Free PDF:
www.lifeplanningtools.link/howtodecide

Kindle ebook for 99 cents:
https://www.amazon.com/dp/B09SYGWRVL/

Ebook

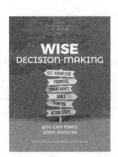

Free PDF

Make Thoughtful Decisions!
Timeless Wisdom. Practical Steps. Lasting Change.

*The Life Planning Series
provides real-life tools
for wise decision-making
and personal transformation*

*Wisdom to Decide.
Steps to Succeed.
Life Starts Here!*

Chapter 1 – Introduction

Life Planning Based on Wisdom!
Build Wisdom. Build Life!

We want to inform, encourage, and inspire you to choose character and improve your life.

The second and equally important purpose is to help you implement specific changes in your life.

Our third goal is to encourage you to pass it on. It is our desire that you will not only obtain this knowledge, but pass it on to others – particularly friends, children, grandchildren, or students.

An African proverb says, *"Don't spend all day rejoicing on your bench. When you pray, move your feet!"* The message of this proverb is that if you want to accomplish something, nothing will happen if you're sitting on your bench all day.

Growth and improvement, including living a better life, requires action and intentionality. The good news is that you can use the information in this book to acquire knowledge that will help you follow a path to a better life.

Those who want to develop a _total life plan_ can do that by acquiring our *Life Planning Handbook*. We will discuss that book later in this chapter.

WHY READ THIS BOOK

The ideal reader of this book is someone who wants to accomplish any of the following:

- learn more about this subject,
- improve your life circumstances,
- live a better life with less stress,
- dig more deeply into the meaning of this subject and how it might impact your life,
- overcome the chaos of life, family or work relationships, or
- learn how to make good or better decisions.

PERSONAL GROWTH

We encourage you to make good choices and improve your personal and family life. This process is often referred to as personal growth or personal development. There are many good reasons for pursuing personal growth in your life:

- to find personal peace, meaning, and purpose,
- to gain more control over life situations,
- to acquire certain skills or abilities,
- to become more disciplined,
- to improve or overcome negative attitudes,
- to expand your horizons,
- to make better decisions,
- to open new avenues of understanding, or
- to change certain outcomes in your life.

It is our hope that this book will help you identify conditions in your life you would like to improve. You may need only some help focusing on the right things. You may just want guidance in finding things you can tweak to make a few changes in your lifestyle. You may want a clearer vision of your goals. Or you may want to do some serious work on some particular aspect of your life. Our Life Planning Series will help you achieve any of these goals and desires.

About *CHOOSE A Positive Self-Image*

This book will help you unlock the power of self-worth and live with confidence, purpose, and joy.

Do you ever feel like you're not enough—or struggle to define who you really are? It's time to stop living by labels, limitations, or the opinions of others. Your true identity isn't found in your appearance, career, past mistakes, or social status—it's built on something far deeper, more powerful, and unshakably personal.

Choose a Positive Self-Image is your roadmap to discovering and embracing your authentic self. With timeless wisdom, practical steps, and empowering insight, this book will help you stop the cycle of self-doubt and start living with confidence, clarity, and emotional freedom.

Inside this life-changing guide, you'll learn how to:

- Break free from the lies and labels that hold you back
- Build a strong, lasting sense of identity and self-worth
- Improve emotional resilience and stability
- Boost your health, relationships, and decision-making
- Align your self-image with truth—not trends or trauma

You'll discover why self-image isn't just about confidence—it's the foundation of better choices, deeper relationships, and a more fulfilled life. Whether you've struggled with insecurity, criticism, failure, or identity confusion, this book gives you the tools to rewrite your story and walk boldly in who you were always meant to be.

You are not your past. You are not your pain. You are more than enough. It's time to believe in who you are—and live like it.

THE LIFE PLANNING SERIES

The Life Planning Series covers most of the important subjects that you would address in an attempt to live a good or better life. Most of the books address one particular subject, help you identify your life goals, and guide you in creating action plans to achieve those goals. One exception is the Life Planning Handbook which will help you develop a complete life plan.

The Series in total addresses such topics as integrity, choosing friends, guarding your speech, working with diligence, making sound financial decisions, having a positive self- image, leadership, faith, choosing core values, and love and family.

Core values of The Life Planning Series

The Life Planning books are developed around ten core values and principles:

1. Wise sayings, parables, proverbs, common sense, and street smarts provide an underlying foundation for gaining knowledge, understanding, and wisdom.

2. Honesty, integrity, and living a life based on truth are the foundational character traits for achieving a life of hope and contentment. They are the cornerstones to living a better life.

3. There are five Primary Life Principles:

- be honest, live with integrity, and base your life on truth,
- choose your friends wisely,
- choose your words carefully,
- be a diligent and hard worker, and
- make sound financial choices.

4. Life change is possible. You can make positive changes and expect good results to follow, but all choices have consequences.

5. It is not necessary to change a large number of character traits in order to achieve significant life improvement. Changing a few *key* areas can have a major impact on your quality of life.

6. The key to making any life change is *intentionality*.

7. Perfection is not possible, but if you aim for it, you can achieve significant results. Nothing will be attained if you do not try.

8. We will be open about the difficulties, barriers, and walls that you might experience in implementing life change. Understand that barriers can be torn down.

9. The ultimate purpose in this series is to develop an effective plan for improving life circumstances. It is not our intent to provide lengthy textbooks on the particular subjects. Our presentation of the text material will be limited to what you need to know in order to develop an effective plan to improve your life.

10. Life is a progressive journey requiring good choices and a solid foundation for the future. Time is needed to implement change. Patience and perseverance will be necessary to achieve the desired results.

Transform Your thinking.
Transform Your Life!

THE BOOKS

Go to the Life Planning Series page
to choose the book you want:

https://www.amazon.com/dp/B09TH9SYC4

THE LIFE PLANNING HANDBOOK

This is a unique book in the Life Planning Series. The purpose is to produce a total and complete *Life Plan* for your life. The sections include:

1. Life Principles and Character Attributes
2. Habits
3. Friends and Family Relationships
4. Work and Work Ethic
5. Education
6. Community Service
7. Money and Wealth
8. Health
9. Spiritual

The planning process in the Handbook will examine your skills and abilities, your personal life values, priorities, and commitments. The book will help you identify your life goals and create action steps to achieve those goals.

This book will generate purpose, direction, and growth in your life.

Go to https://www.amazon.com/dp/1952359325
to get your copy now.

Decision Fatigue Ends Here!

A structured approach to turn wisdom into results.

Chapter 2
Consequences

"Mess with the bull and
one usually gets the horns."
Latin American saying[3]

GENERAL

Consequences are a vital concept in our understanding of making good choices and setting goals to have a successful life. Thus, this chapter on consequences will appear in most of the books in the Life Planning Series.

You have complete freedom to choose what you want to do, but you cannot choose the consequences. Thus, poor choices can be a disaster. We bear the consequences of our words and actions. It is like a law of nature.

A teenager, constantly trying to meet social expectations, begins to lose touch with who he really is. Only after turning inward and identifying his personal values does he gain peace and clarity. When your identity is rooted in your core values, not the surrounding crowd, you find stability that fame, popularity, or appearance can't provide.

If you don't want to suffer the negative results of poor decisions, think in advance what your actions are likely to produce. What you do and what you say will have lasting impact on yourself and on others.

THERE WILL BE CONSEQUENCES

Life is a series of decisions and choices. We are constantly making choices about both significant and insignificant things. Choices shape the course of our lives. Some people learn a great deal from the consequences of their actions and others seem oblivious.

Consider the woman who bases her confidence on compliments and social media likes. When the praise stops, so does her self-esteem. Eventually, she learns to affirm her worth through purposeful living and real relationships. External validation fades—but internal self-worth carries you through every season of life.

Physical consequences are a law of nature. If you touch a hot stove you will get burned. If you walk into the street in front of a truck you will be injured. Behaviors have predictable consequences as well. If you cheat and lie, people will stop doing business with you and your reputation will suffer. If you are not dependable, people will no longer trust you.

By definition consequences occur as a result of something else happening. The result may occur immediately or it could take a while, even years. This is often one of the reasons that we make poor choices – the consequence does not occur immediately and because of this we think there will never be consequences.

The actual consequences you experience will vary depending on your circumstances, but there will be consequences nonetheless. The degree or size of the consequence will also vary, but we should not be fooled into thinking small transgressions have no consequences.

*"One who steals has no right
to complain if he is robbed."*
Aesop[4]

THE FARMER AND THE OX

There was a farmer who had been plowing hard for many days with an ox and mule yoked together. The ox told the mule that they should pretend to be sick and rest. The mule declined saying, "No, we must get the work done, for the season is short." But the ox played sick and the farmer brought him hay and corn and made him comfortable.

When the mule came in from plowing the ox asked how things had gone. The mule said, "We didn't get as much done but we did okay, I guess." The ox asked, "Did the old man say anything about me?" Nothing," said the mule. The next day the ox played sick again. When the tired mule came in he asked again how it went. "All right, but we sure didn't get much done." The ox asked, "What did the old man say about me?" The mule replied, "Nothing directly to me, but he had a long talk with the butcher."[5]

This is similar to the message in the story concerning the consequences of a hearty breakfast to the chicken and the pig. A breakfast of ham and eggs to the chicken is a temporary inconvenience, but to the pig it is a permanent and lasting consequence – breakfast is a <u>real</u> commitment.

All actions have consequences!

COUNT THE COST

Someone has said that you will ultimately be invited to a party where you will dine on your own consequences.

Whether your actions were wise or unwise, you will eventually bear the consequences. Thus, it is important to think about the consequences in advance. What will result from your words or actions?

Regardless of the particular situation, it will always be easier to arrive at a positive outcome if you have thought ahead, evaluated the circumstances, and determined in advance how you will respond to the important challenges that arise in your life.

After a career setback, a man feels lost and unsure of who he is without his title. Through reflection and effort, he begins to redefine himself by his integrity, core values, and real friends. When you let your job define your worth, you forfeit your identity to circumstances. When you build on internal values, no loss can undo you.

What you do and say in questionable circumstances will have a lasting impact on your life. Emblazon the following truth in your mind and on your heart:

> *Consequences shape lives.*
> *Choices produce consequences*
> *which direct the course of life.*
> *Therefore, count the cost!*

LEGACY

Our words and actions can have an impact for a long time. The ongoing impact of poor behavior is a concept that escapes many people. Poor decisions can affect a family for many generations. Bad behavior establishes a pattern that becomes the blueprint for a child's future behavior.

A young woman, bombarded with unrealistic beauty standards, believes she's not good enough. One day, she begins journaling her strengths, fostering gratitude, and embracing self-care. Over time, her self-image shifts. Confronting false narratives and choosing truth leads to a more confident and grounded life. Adopting the standards of society, false narratives, and sometimes family and even friends can lead you down a path to despair.

Your legacy extends into future generations; therefore, be sure that it is a positive one! Most people have no concept of how their behavior can impact the future. This is dramatically demonstrated by comparing the lives of Jonathan Edwards and Max Jukes.

Jonathan Edwards was a Puritan preacher in the 1700s. His descendants demonstrate the powerful influence of wise choices and a godly life. At the turn of the 20th century, A. E. Winship decided to trace the descendants of Jonathan Edwards and compare them to a man known as Max Jukes.

Mr. Jukes was incarcerated in the New York prison system at the time Jonathan Edwards was preaching. Winship found that 42 of the men in the New York prison system could trace their heritage back to Max Jukes. Jukes, an atheist, lived a godless life. He married an ungodly woman, and from the descendants of this union 310 died as paupers, 150 were criminals, 7 were murderers, and more than half of the women were prostitutes.

In contrast, the record of Jonathan Edwards' progeny tells a much different story. An investigation of 1,394 known descendants of Jonathan Edwards revealed

- 13 college presidents,
- 65 college professors,
- 3 United States Senators,

- 30 judges,
- 100 lawyers,
- 60 physicians,
- 75 army and navy officers,
- 100 preachers and missionaries,
- 60 authors of prominence,
- 1 Vice-President of the United States,
- 80 public officials in other capacities,
- 295 college graduates.

Today, instead of the blessings like those that came to Jonathan Edwards' progeny, we are seeing a growing multitude like the descendants of Max Jukes! Have you seen a family in which the grandfather was an alcoholic – and his sons and grandsons abuse alcohol, too? Have you seen a family plagued with sickness, drug abuse, debt, or poverty? Often that is because someone in the past did not make good choices. We are going to leave a legacy for our children and grandchildren. Will we pass on a blessing or a curse?[8]

Your actions, both good and bad, establish the foundation of your life, lifestyle, and legacy.

We reap what we sow

In a number of his proverbs, King Solomon suggests that doing what is right is to be preferred over evil. King Solomon was known world-wide for his great wisdom. He wrote and recorded many proverbs recognized for their practical insight and wisdom. He describes the nature of righteousness as being immovable and that it will stand above evil.

Is your desire for doing what is "right" rooted deeply or is it planted in shallow soil that can easily be washed away? Solomon indicated that the wicked would ultimately be overthrown and that the righteous would survive because their character had roots that were deep and impossible to dislodge.

Solomon argued that it is better to be on the side of the righteous. The reasoning is the same as the man who chooses to build his house, business, or life on rock versus sand. If we build on sand (questionable ways) then our hopes and plans will never stand up against the storms of life. If we build on rock (high character) our plans should hold firm.

We do reap what we sow and if we sow badly because we have rejected what is right, the wise counsel of friends, or ethical core values, we will reap the negative consequences. Those who think they know everything frequently reject wisdom and follow their own plans and schemes. It has been said that those who insist on following their poorly chosen ways will often end up choking on them.

Lysa Terkeurst in her book, *The Best Yes,* says this about making decisions: "The decision you make determines the schedule you keep. The schedule you keep determines the life you live. And how you live your life determines how you spend your soul."

Think about that statement. You could say this truth in a number of ways – Ms. Terkeurst chose this particular description. But any way you say it the meaning is, *your decisions determine your life*. The consequences of your decisions constitute your day and your future. You are always living in the midst of the choices you make; therefore, make good choices. The consequences will determine how you live your life, or in Terkeurst's words, how you "spend your soul."

Think about the man raised in a broken home who believed he was destined to repeat the past. But as he chose new mentors and healthier relationships, he began to rewrite his identity based on positive input. Where you come from may shape your story, but who you become is determined by the choices you make today.

IT'S NOT FAIR

Unfortunately, life is not fair. Worrying about fairness, arguing about it, or fighting it will be of little value. Being "fair" generally means that everyone is treated equally (the concept of socialism). But life is not fair!
If you believe that life is intended to be fair, then it's not fair to others less fortunate that you were born in America and are therefore privileged. It is not fair that you have avoided poverty, wars, terrorism, natural disasters, tyrants, dying in an accident, abuse . . .

Obviously it is unrealistic to argue it's not fair that we experience the consequences of our own poor choices, especially since we are the ones making those poor choices. If we think we shouldn't incur the result of our poor choices then we certainly should not expect to experience the rewards of our good choices.

Consider the woman in midlife who questions her purpose as her roles and routines shift. She could spiral—but instead, she embraces the chance to evolve, exploring new passions and deepening her character. Life changes don't erase your identity; they invite you to strengthen and redefine it.

*Think about the consequences,
then choose wisely!*

WHO TO BLAME

Blame is a big concern for many people today. When something bad happens, the first reaction by many is to find someone to blame. Many people no longer accept the concept of an "accident." It's become the cultural norm to assign blame and "make someone pay."

Some of us react in illogical ways to consequences. The most illogical is the person who totally ignores the obvious dangers of what they are about to do and then rather than accepting the consequences, casts blame. They become angry or embarrassed and attempt to find someone or something to blame in order to take the attention off their own poor judgment.

Taking responsibility for mistakes, misunderstandings, or accidents is becoming a lost art. Many children have been raised to believe they do not have to suffer consequences.

MISTAKES!

What happens when we make a mistake? A mistake is not the end of the world – it's a mistake, not a death sentence! If we make a wrong choice, we must rethink the issue and select another path. We all make mistakes. The real challenge in life is how we handle those mistakes.

Not every choice we make will be the right decision. Expect some failures in life and don't be overwhelmed if what you choose does not work out as you expect. If the choice was bad, wrong, or ill-advised, fix it!

If you always try to please others you will become someone who doesn't know what he believes. Commit to living authentically, grounded in your faith, core values, and truth. Authenticity may cost you approval at times, but it rewards you with clarity, purpose, and peace.

Admitting mistakes and taking responsibility
is a characteristic of those who
are living their best life.

BARRIERS

Difficulties and barriers can be overcome if you are determined to find a solution. It's a lot easier to make changes in life if you are receiving guidance and help. In addition to our books we suggest finding someone to join you in improving your life circumstances. If you cannot find someone to participate with you, find someone you can meet with weekly or periodically to discuss your progress, your difficulties, your needs, and most of all, your successes.

Here are some effective ways to overcome personal barriers:

1. Recognize that many barriers are in reality just excuses.
2. Recruit a support person (friend) to hold you accountable.
3. Recruit others to do it with you.
4. Recruit support from your family.
5. If time is a hurdle – work it out. Adjust your schedule and priorities.

Do not expect change, improvement, or miracles overnight. Ask for help when you need it.

"Being challenged in life is inevitable,
being defeated is optional."
Roger Crawford[9]

TIPS TO AVOID UNINTENDED CONSEQUENCES

Here are five tips you could adopt before making decisions:

1. **THINK** before you act.
   > Take time to consider the consequences.
   > Ask yourself, "What would 'wisdom' do?"
   > Think logically.

2. **LISTEN** to the advice of others.
   > Seek out trusted friends.

3. **CONSIDER** the pros and cons.
   > How will this decision impact me or others?
   > Will I be proud of the outcome?
   > What would my friends think?

4. **BE PATIENT**.
   > "Sleep on it" is often excellent advice.
   > Research as much as you can.

5. **EMOTIONS** often cause poor decisions.
   > Base your choices on facts and reality, not feelings.
   > Do not make decisions based on your emotions.

TIPS YOU COULD USE

a. Underline, circle, or highlight the tips above or anything in this chapter that you think could make the most impact if you implemented them in your life. You will revisit these choices at the end of the book in the Planning section.

b. There may be other things that you think would make a difference. Write them below:

_____

_____

_____

_____

"It is the peculiar quality of a fool to perceive the faults of others and to forget his own."
Cicero[10]

"A strong, positive self-image is the best possible preparation for success."

Joyce Brothers[11]

Chapter 3
Identity Life Principle

*Your character and your life begin with a
blank slate. Life is what you make it.*

WHAT'S THE FOUNDATION OF WHO I AM?

You are the sum total of all your characteristics and your
actions. The foundation of your identity lies within your
inner being. It is a combination of your core values, the
moral standards you have adopted, how you view your
purpose in life, and even your basic beliefs about right-
wrong and good-evil.

Having a solid foundation in your life makes it much easier
to address or deal with your identity. Many fall into the
trap of thinking their identity and value come from their
performance, job, relationships, and many other factors
that influence and affect our lives.

There are world-views that believe people are inherently
"good." I find that position very difficult to support.
Responsible parents spend a great deal of time and effort
teaching their children good behavior: don't take toys that
are not yours, don't hit or bite people, tell the truth, etc.
No one ever has to teach a toddler to grab a toy from a
friend (or a store shelf), to hit or bite, or to lie to escape a

31

consequence. That bad behavior is already inherently present in children. We do not arrive in this world with inherent goodness, kindness, forgiveness, or love. We must be taught to be good.

SELF-IDENTITY

Self-identity is a term that means or describes how you think about or view yourself. Remember, your self-identity or self-image can change as your life changes, as you grow in understanding and stature, as others impact your life in important ways, and as you deal with and overcome the challenges of life.

Some situations in your life can change dramatically and even disappear simply because your life changes. Others may take on different meaning as you engage in new or challenging life situations.

Self-identity can be influenced (both good and bad) by the views and descriptions placed on us by others. Our self-identity may experience a number of highs and lows as we live our lives. It will not be static.

This book is about self: your self-image, self-identity, self-esteem, self-worth, self-value, etc. It is about who you think you are, regardless of what you say or do. Identity is not a function of what you look like, where you work, or your wealth. But these factors and many more all come together to _influence_ how you see and feel about yourself. Thus, your identity is defined by the unique characteristics (physical, psychological, and interpersonal), that make up and describe who you are.

How identity develops.

Your identity is formed by many different factors, behaviors, and roles, as well as from how you interact with others. In an effort to simplify identity, some experts have said that our identity is formed from three major areas of life: occupation, beliefs and values, and sexuality.

But our identity is also fluid because:

- We may be actively investigating certain beliefs and have not yet reached a conclusion.
- We have not made any commitment to certain beliefs and values and feel uncomfortable in a world where others have made such decisions and commitments.
- We change our commitment to certain values or beliefs as we mature.
- We may not have fully investigated certain beliefs or values, and as we gain knowledge and understanding our identity becomes consistent with this new knowledge.

How does a poor self-image develop?

A poor or distorted self-image is not uncommon in our society, particularly in large and robust economies, societies, and capitalist cultures. Low self-esteem or poor self-image can be troubling in business, personal relationships, and reaching ultimate life contentment.

The good news is that there are steps you can take to improve your self-image and raise your self-esteem. We will include many tips and suggestions in this book for improving your self-image. If you suffer from low self-esteem, take heart: you can make significant improvements by implementing a few simple steps that will make important positive changes in your self-image.

The key to all self-improvement is intentionality. You must first acknowledge that change is necessary and then you must care enough to take action to change how you define yourself.

> *"No one can make you feel inferior*
> *without your consent."*
> Eleanor Roosevelt[12]

SELF-IMAGE

What is self-image?

Self-image and identity go by various and often similar terms: self-esteem, self-worth, self-confidence, self-respect, etc. Self-image has nothing to do with what you see in a mirror, but it has a great deal to do with what you *think* when you look in the mirror. Self-image relates to what we think of ourselves when we think about who we are. Yes, it may have some reference to physical appearance, but the inner qualities and beliefs are the key to your real identity.

Merriam-Webster defines self-image as, "one's conception of oneself or of one's role." It also describes it as the way you think about yourself, your abilities, and appearance. Synonyms include any term that describes your perception of self.

Self-image might logically be explained as the life experiences that have taken place over time to create a perception of self as it relates to reality. Those experiences can produce both positive and negative thoughts and actions. They can give confidence or cause you to doubt. How you summarize all that and describe what you think of yourself defines your self-image.

> *"The 'self-image' is the key to human*
> *personality and human behavior.*
> *Change the self-image and you*
> *change the personality and the behavior."*
> Maxwell Maltz[13]

A positive self-image can be described as when:

- You see yourself as attractive and desirable.
- You see yourself as smart and intelligent.
- You see yourself as happy and healthy.
- You see yourself as successful.
- You see yourself as able to overcome obstacles and find solutions.
- You see yourself as unaware of negative influences.

A negative self-image may look like the reverse of the positive descriptions above. You may think of yourself as unattractive, unintelligent, unhappy, and even a failure.

> *The key to a life well lived is*
> *to have an honest view of self.*

CONCEPTS OF YOUR SELF-IMAGE

Although there is no one specific definition of what defines your self-image, there are some widely used descriptions that can be used to outline what it means to most people. It is often described as:

- How you think or feel about yourself.
- How you believe others think about you.
- How you want to be perceived by others.

Within these categories there may be questions or issues concerning:

- personality,
- Intelligence,
- business and technical skills,
- social skills, and
- moral principles and core values.

Within these concepts you can think about your own situation and gain a reasonably good understanding of your personal self-image status.

RESULTS OF NEGATIVE SELF-IMAGE ISSUES

Negative self-image issues are often described as a distorted self-image. People feel they are not worthy, not good, and even consider themselves failures. The result is often anxiety or depression. Relationships are often tenuous or at best very difficult.

Most experts believe that a positive self-image is absolutely necessary to have contentment and satisfaction in life. People who have a positive self-image are usually successful, happy, and confident, and normally have close and lasting relationships. What is the status of your identity or self-image? Do you feel good about yourself or do you consider yourself a failure? You are probably somewhere between those two situations.

Life is uncertain. Therefore, if you define yourself by one primary aspect of life and things go bad in that area, your whole life may begin to crumble. For example, if you define yourself in terms of your job, company, or career and you lose your job, your life is likely turned upside down for a period of time. It may take months to find a new job. You may have to change occupations. This will tend to devastate your life if you define your worth primarily in terms of your job or career.

We used an example of your occupation above, but it could be any other area in your life you have adopted to define your identity. It might be family or relationships, your children, your health, or your wealth. If you define yourself by your wealth and you go broke, your life will be in a shambles until you are able to recognize that these "things" do not define your worth or value.

If you rely on outside uncontrollable influences to determine your self-image and identity, your life can be in chaos for an extended period. It can even take years to recover self-esteem if you base your self-worth on a particular area of life that changed dramatically.

SELF-ESTEEM

Self-esteem is a term that is often used interchangeably with self-image. However, self-esteem goes deeper than self-image. Self-esteem includes the sense of honor or respect we have for ourselves and indicates if that is good or bad. If we have a poor self-image it will strongly influence our self-esteem. If we have low self-esteem, it will likely be accompanied by a negative self-image.

*"Nobody holds a good opinion of a man
who holds a low opinion of himself."*
Anthony Trollope[14]

Identity is a more comprehensive description or term compared to self-image. Identity is the *totality* of who we are. Thus, identity is the whole person and the definition of who we believe ourselves to be. Self-image is only a portion of that description. Roy Baumeister describes identity as follows: *"The term 'identity' refers to the definitions that are created for and superimposed on the self."*[15]

Self-esteem can change due to both internal and external factors. Personal feelings have a significant impact on the way a person feels about himself. Low self-esteem can produce worry, anxiety, and even depression. If you have low self-esteem you are likely to feel uncomfortable around others, shy, and even insecure in important life functions.

Positive individuals are confident about their skills and abilities. They will tend to assert their confidence in ways that define their self-identity. But someone who has low self-esteem is not likely to consider himself worthy of his current status or a future status which may be on the horizon.

EVENTS THAT CAUSE PERSONAL IDENTITY ISSUES

There are many examples that might be cited on how someone's self-identify can be impacted over time or on an immediate basis. Identity is particularly vulnerable to major life changes. For example:

Adopting, changing, or committing fully to a religion

Changing your religion or level of commitment normally involves changing values. Such a change may cause a significant impact on your self-identity. For example, converting to Christianity requires belief in their doctrines and living in a manner consistent with that faith.

Earning a college degree

When you become a lawyer, doctor, teacher, or actuary after completing a difficult course of study, your self-identity will change from student to professional. College graduates have additional privileges compared to ongoing students. But those privileges also have responsibilities that must or should be fulfilled. Professionals have inherent obligations and status placed on them by the business world and the culture.

Public service

Serving in public office brings both privileges and obligations. A certain level of competence is expected with the granting of the privileges of public office. Service in public office can bring criticism. This can cause self-doubt, which can impact self-esteem if positive results are not produced in the job.

CONCLUSION

If we keep an honest view of ourselves and the world around us, it becomes easier to maintain an honest or proper understanding of who we are. We have issues or sometimes a full-blown crisis when we begin seeing the world differently and begin questioning our value, worth, or purpose.

Developing a strong sense of identity that is positive and encouraging will make your life journey much easier. We will likely have serious life problems if we have constant anxiety about our place in the world. It is particularly important for teenagers and young adults who may be questioning their place in life for the first time.

However, our self-image and identity will change as we mature and grow in knowledge and understanding. Thus, self-image problems can occur at any age or stage of life.

The formation of self-image and self-identity is one of the most important developments that individuals must deal with as they mature. Our identity evolves and so must we. But we need a foundation of morals, priorities, and core values that remain relatively constant throughout life.

A positive self-image is the result of work and focus, not neglect, worry, and apathy.

Wisdom to Action Challenge

Reflect on your core values. Are they guiding your decisions? Identify one area where you can live more intentionally, strengthening your self-image and overcoming challenges.

Chapter 4
What Determines Your Identity?

"If you want light to come into your life,
you need to stand where it is shining."
Guy Finley[16]

The simple answer to the question of what determines your identity is, "*You* do." But that answer is probably not of any real help if you have self-image problems.

Our purpose in this chapter is to briefly discuss the *many* factors that influence your self-image and identity.

Because of the large number of components that could have an effect on your identity, you might think that everything in your environment will influence your self-image. You would be generally accurate in drawing that conclusion. Almost everything we do will have some influence. But some influences are far stronger and more important than others.

These influences are important to understand because they can create serious problems, feelings, and perceptions about yourself and others that are not necessarily true. If you are seeking to determine who you are and how and why you are unique, these influences can prevent the development of a positive and secure self-identity. There can be confusion about gender, sexual

41

identity, culture, or ethnic considerations that make understanding your identity difficult. You may be confused, frustrated, or even excluded by others based on your own perception of your identity.

These feelings and perceptions often result from a lack of good parental guidance in your childhood, true friends, or mentors in your life. The absence of these influences can lead to low self-esteem and feeling no one cares about you. These feelings will generally have a negative impact on your self-image.

DETERMINING FACTORS

The following factors will ultimately influence or even determine how you live your life. They will influence your ethics and moral standards. The standards you adopt will lead to real world actions. They will determine how you act and what you do.

In order to discuss these factors we have separated them into two groups: those that we can control and those that we generally cannot control. For example, your parents and family will have a great influence on your identity, but you cannot choose your parents and family. Yes, you can control how you react to their influence, but you will absorb their impact on your identity and can do very little to avoid their influence.

Note that in some categories both factors exist: those we can control and those we cannot control. For example, in the area of relationships, we have no control over who our parents will be but we do have control over who we choose as a spouse.

INFLUENCES: Those things over which we have control

A. RELATIONSHIPS: spouse, friends
The people in your life will influence your values, standards, likes, and dislikes to a great extent. You are around people all the time and the values and beliefs of friends, family, and co-workers will have a great impact on your self-image. You choose your spouse, friends, and associates. Do it wisely.

B. WORK: job, career, employer
Our self-image may suffer a significant shock when we begin our work life. Attitudes and goals are not the same at work as that in the home. You need to perform and in fact, perform at an adequate level or you could be fired. Even if you perform well, you may lose your job if the business is not doing well or not run well. You must please your employer and immediate bosses or you won't have a job. Co-workers will take interest in you and form opinions about you or your work because there is a degree of interdependence between you and your co-workers. Poor work by one person can severely impact others.

C. LOCATION: country, state, city, urban, rural
The person who grows up in a busy, noisy, or dangerous city environment will have different influences than one who grows up in a rural farming community where nature, hard work, care for animals or food crops is the environment and primary source of income. The perspective about life is totally different. One environment is not necessarily better than the other, but they will teach different values, beliefs, and work ethic.

D. INFLUENCERS: mentors, heroes, books, songs
You can choose many of the things that might influence your life, your thinking, and your identity. You can choose

your heroes, mentors, and friends. You can choose books and music that deliver a positive message. You don't have to listen to songs that degrade people. You don't have to read trashy books.

E. HEALTH – Addictions: drugs, alcohol, sex, work, fitness
You have complete control over your lifestyle. You can choose to eat healthy foods and engage in exercise. You can choose to drive safely. You have control over the substances you put into your body such as tobacco, alcohol, and drugs. You have control over your sexual behavior. Wise decisions in these areas will have a huge impact on the way others see you and the way you see yourself.

F. WEALTH: rich, destitute, well-off, poor
The amount and nature of your wealth will have a significant impact on your identity. If you earned it yourself you will have certain feeling of pride and self-worth. If you won it in a lottery or were given the gift of a trust fund when you reached age 21, you will have a much different perspective about such wealth. You choose to allow wealth to have either a good or bad influence on your life. Others will influence your identity by the way they treat you because of wealth. Don't let wealth or lack thereof control your life, determine your core values, or dictate your character. You must control the influences of wealth.

G. SPIRITUAL: religion, beliefs, church
You are the one who chooses what you believe. You should learn in advance what is expected if you join a religious group. Your image can be greatly influenced by your beliefs. Guilt is often the result of not performing in the expected manner. Others may not necessarily know about these failures but you do.

H. CORE VALUES: purpose, mission, morals, life priorities
Your core values are totally in your control, but they can
be influenced by others. Therefore, surround yourself with
people whose core values you admire, and then be sure
that you are the one determining your core values.

I. CHARACTER: attitudes, habits, behavior, reputation
Just like core values, you must determine the nature of
your character and the attitudes and habits that result. If
you don't like the results you can change your personal
character, but that is not always easy if habits are firmly
established. Just like a negative self-image that might
result from poor character, it may take a lot of work to
change once you have chosen the wrong path. But be
assured that you can change, if you are intentional.

J. DEPENDENCE: controlled, free, self-reliant
If you are controlled or enslaved by some entity, person,
cause, or idea, remember, you are the one who chose it.
You can change it by exercising your own personal choice.
Don't allow others to determine your values, your words,
or your actions. If you are an adult, you are free and not
dependent on anyone else for anything, unless you choose
it or allow it.

K. LIFESTYLE:
You choose the lifestyle you live. If you don't like it or
don't enjoy it, change it. Your lifestyle should cater to you,
not to others. If you want quiet stillness surrounded by
nature, you will not find that on the streets of New York.
Go where you want to go and do what you want to do
because it will greatly influence your well-being and be a
positive influence on your self-image.

L. CAUSES: charities, politics
You choose these causes. If you don't like them once you
are involved, quit.

INFLUENCES: Things over which we have no control

M. RELATIONSHIPS: parents, co-workers
You have no control over the parents you have and
generally no control over your co-workers, although you
can choose not to work for a company where you know
the workers or working conditions are not good.

N. FAMILY: family, relatives . . . characterized by love,
caring, and respect, or neglect and abuse
Your family (or care giver) has a large impact on your self-
image. During your formative years you are absorbing
their values, beliefs, and standards. It is impossible not to
be influenced by the family unit. As you get older you may
determine that what you learned about yourself from
family members was not true. It may take some serious
effort to change your way of thinking about yourself.

Another characteristic of family influence is that because it
comes from people you trust and love, you think that it
must be true. It can be very traumatic when you realize
that family members were wrong and may have even been
hurtful.

O. UPBRINGING – Life Story: successes, failures
Your upbringing and what you were taught by family,
teachers, and mentors will have significant impact on your
life story. Much of life is determined by what you do and
what you hear before the age of thirteen. By that time
your life story is well established. If your upbringing was
not helpful in establishing a solid self-identity, you may

have ongoing self-image problems. You may need professional help to overcome those early negative influences.

*"It's like everyone tells a story
about themselves inside their own head.
That story makes you what you are.
We build ourselves out of that story."*
Gabriel García Márquez[17]

P. HEALTH: wellness, fitness
Your self-image and even your identity can be impacted by your state of health. If you do not have the strength or stamina to do a job, do your chores, or hold up your end of any other responsibilities, others may be frustrated or unforgiving by your performance. Serious health problems may affect your whole identity. People with disabilities may have particular difficulties because their life and identity is often influenced by their disability.

Q. HUMAN CHARACTERISTICS: size, shape, condition, gender, skin color
Although it is not logical, your size and shape will influence your own self-image and the image others have of you. We are constantly bombarded with images of perfection by influencers and TV commercials. We are stuck with this idiocy and must simply do our best to overcome the negative self-image it produces.

R. WORK: bosses, co-workers
We have no control over who our supervisors and co-workers will be, other than in choosing our employer. These people can be very influential in determining and defining our self-image because we spend significant amounts of time at work.

SUMMARY

Thus, we are, by many definitions, creatures of our environment. Some things we can control and others we cannot. As we mature and are exposed to different life factors we may feel pressure to change our self-image or identity. We come to realize that there are competing influences and we have the ability to choose what is right for us.

We might also discover that we have made incorrect choices. The influences on our self-image that occurred from a particular source may no longer be very strong and they may prove to be inappropriate. Therefore, we change our self-image and ultimately our identity.

"Don't ever compare yourself to others.
You are not a copy, you are an original.
Craft your own individuality and sense of
style and just be yourself. Trying to be
someone else will only frustrate you
and make you unhappy and miserable."
Yvonne I Wilson[18]

Wisdom to Action Challenge

Evaluate your relationships. Are you actively selecting influences that align with your purpose? Identify one external dependency you can reduce this week, focusing on internal values and maintaining authenticity.

Chapter 5
Understanding Your Identity and Self-image

*"To love oneself is the beginning
of a lifelong romance."*
Oscar Wilde[19]

People tend to experience an identity crisis during *stressful* seasons in their life. These are usually times of great change and upheaval. A crisis is very likely whenever one must enter something that is outside their comfort zone. These times might be the:

- moving to a new and unknown location, particularly far away from friends and family;
- beginning of a new job, which may have followed the loss of employment;
- death of a friend or family member;
- learning about a serious health condition;
- beginning or ending of a serious relationship;
- birth or loss of a child; or
- loss of wealth.

Remember that you are a work in progress and your identity is always changing, even by small amounts. It may change dramatically as the result of larger and significant events like those listed above.

An important question is, "How is your self-image or identity impacting your life?" Is your good, bad, or indifferent view of yourself affecting your life, your work, or your relationships? Is a poor self-image or low self-esteem impacting your life in good or bad ways?

What do you tend to do about negative and positive areas of your life? Do you worry about them or do you ignore them? How do you cope or live with them on a daily basis? Are you just accepting your perceived status or are you consciously trying to change something? Are you winning or losing these battles? Can you define or identify the circumstances that are creating self-image problems?

What is the primary influence in your life that drives your identity? Do you have control over that influence or do you feel helpless? Remember, you have inherent abilities that you can use to make changes in your life and shape your identity. You can change your self-image and overcome those influences that are holding you back. But such change may be difficult and could stretch your ability to cope.

You have certain skills, gifts, and abilities. What are they producing in your life? Have you allowed negative self-talk to hold you back from achieving goals? What are you currently producing in your life? Have you invested adequate time in the important facets of life – things that have lasting or eternal value?

The good news is that you can improve self-image and identity issues through hard work, diligence, good friends, and positive self-talk. But you must be intentional.

CAUSES OF LOW SELF-ESTEEM

We have defined self-esteem as how you feel about your value or worth. Following are reasons that might produce low self-esteem.

No power or influence

People who feel they have no influence or importance will often suffer from self-image issues. A person who is never included in anything important or who is excluded when decisions are being made is likely to feel worthless and not accepted by family, friends, or even society.

This can occur because of your gender, race, ethnicity, or economic status. It might be because of any number of factors, many of which are out of your control. Unfortunately, most people who are in the middle of these situations think the problem is some inadequacy in their own makeup. The truth is that it is typically not about them personally but the result of a changing society and culture that puts great importance on self and personal importance to the detriment of others.

Distorted self-Image

A distorted self-image means that you view yourself in a way that is not based on reality. This distortion is often related to body issues that may or may not be real. You may think that you are heavier than you really are and it results in constant dieting and anxiety about your weight. It can lead to a fixation with fitness and exercise which results in excessive amounts of time in the gym or unreasonable dieting.

If you are obsessed with your appearance you may spend large amounts of money trying to cover up or change your appearance with clothing, make-up, hair, etc. Undergoing surgery to change your appearance can be the result of a distorted importance on self-image. Other habits that indicate appearance issues include frequently comparing ourselves to others, repeatedly checking the mirror, or excessive and frequent grooming.

Your problems may more accurately be described as an unstable self-image. You may not know who you are or where you fit. These feelings may vary widely over time. The symptoms of an unstable self-image include:

- Your self-image is not based on reality and your feelings and perceptions vary a great deal from month to month.
- You feel empty.
- You fear rejection.
- You experience mood swings that can last for days.
- You are anxious and suffer depression.
- You act with abandon and are impulsive.
- You make poor or even risky decisions.
- Your relationships go hot and cold.
- You do not feel empathy for others.
- You are frequently bored.
- You become hostile with others.

It should not be surprising that a distorted or poor self-image can result in depression. If you are not happy with who you are or what you are doing, it is easy to fall into a state of depression.

Conversely, a healthy and positive self-image is important for many reasons. A recent study showed that:

1. a) 75% of women considered themselves overweight, but only 25% were actually overweight.
   b) After 70% of the women viewed images of fashion models they felt more depressed and angry than before.
2. The body type of models portrayed as ideal occurs naturally in only 5% of American women.
3. Only 10% of high school students are overweight, but 90% are on some form of diet.
4. Teenagers who engage in unprotected sex, which results in unwanted pregnancy, often have poor self-images.
5. Today's media greatly influences the self-image of individuals, particularly teenagers.[20]

AM I GOOD ENOUGH?

Today individuals are seeking to be free and to dictate the identity they desire. That can be both good and bad. Everyone wants to be their own individual. Formerly we introduced ourselves by the term, "I am so-and-so." Today that is often replaced with "I identify myself as." People think they can determine all aspects of their identity.

Years ago, one's individual identity was the result of actual biological sex, age, and experience. Nationality and culture were strong identifiers. Today a person can choose how to identify *itself*. Modern humans distinguish biological sex from gender.

The phrase "I identify as" creates the illusion that people today are more self-aware. They use mind power and will power in directing their life with "positive thinking." This all sounds freeing, but studies show the devastating reality behind what seems like empowering thoughts. These "freeing" thoughts can leave individuals empty and even more depressed.

Anyone who is bored with his own reality can change to a more desired *virtual* reality. However, this delightful and twisted idea of happiness and freedom involves a considerable amount of danger. Virtual realities are not real. It is easy to become confused by endless realities. Choosing one's own self-reality today is merely the result of social influence, not necessarily any intelligent thought and analysis.

> *"Who am I? They mock me,*
> *these lonely questions of mine."*
> Dietrich Bonhoeffer[21]

BEING YOURSELF

If you lose your sense of identity you will lose your vision of your past, present, and future. That will usually result in a loss of confidence and reality. Reality determines your ability to define your self-worth, have relationships, and experience love.

A positive and stable identity is the foundation of ongoing and durable relationships. If you have self-image issues and a weak self-identity, relationships become more difficult. If you are suffering under the illusion that you lack self-worth your relationships will be strained because you will constantly be concerned about self-image issues.

Social media can often increase tensions if you are dealing with self-image problems. Social media has its own agenda and that is not necessarily your welfare. Comparison of identities over social media is an exercise in futility. Data is frequently manipulated to make one appear something they are not. There is little to be gained by trying to compare yourself, your success, or your opportunities to others on social media.

The solution: be yourself!

> *"To be yourself in a world that is constantly trying to make you something else is the greatest accomplishment."*
> Ralph Waldo Emerson[22]

WHAT IS MY SELF-IMAGE?

Before we discuss how to deal with self-image or identity issues, it is important that we truly understand what self-image is all about. We often use a number of false realities to define ourselves. The most common are:

Our appearance

Too many of us make appearance an important aspect in evaluating our self-worth. But it is a false narrative. The old saying that, "beauty is skin deep" is proven true over and over again. Very few people actually think of themselves as beautiful, and not many more consider themselves attractive.

Unfortunately social media, television, the internet and nearly all advertising and most influencers, sell beauty, attractiveness, and sex. Remember, all the advertising is for the purpose of selling you something. Unfortunately little, if any, of what we see in ads actually represents reality. It is designed to convince you to buy something.

There certainly are attractive people in this world but they are actually a very small percentage of the population and they are not all young. Somehow we seem to have come to equate youth and beauty with wisdom. Any athlete or young successful actor is now considered to be an expert on any number of subjects. We must resist the idea of youth and beauty having some irresistible ability to tell the rest of the world what is right, what is good, and what we should do to be happy.

Your appearance can certainly have some influence on others because it can portray authority, wealth, health, etc. But that is all it does, it gives the appearance of something – it does not necessarily portray reality. Having a reputation in sports or movies does not mean that someone has anything important to say or is worth listening to. They simply have a platform because of their fame or popularity.

Our abilities

People seem to be drawn to individuals who can catch or throw a ball farther than anyone else, even though they may have graduated from high school or college with a "D" average. Paying them large sums of money because of their unique physical talent does not make them statesmen or give them any special understanding or wisdom about politics, social issues, laws, or good investments. It simply gives them a platform.

Our accomplishments

Some people measure their worth by their college degrees, successful careers, or business success. But these successes do not measure value or worth. People with good sales techniques, smooth demeanors, or effective negotiation skills may be able to "sell" their accomplishments to others, but that does not make their conclusions about truth or core values particularly valid.

Accomplishments can be commendable. One should be proud of achievements. But they do not necessarily indicate personal value, wisdom, or truth. Truth is true regardless of who may say it is true or say it is false. We must not be swayed by people who have a platform because of some unrelated accomplishment.

Our possessions

Some try to use their wealth and possessions as leverage. If someone is rich, many automatically think they can be trusted and have important insight. This is not necessarily true. But that's why you see famous people hawking products. The watching and listening public apparently think these people have special insight on any number of subjects.

The public is enamored with famous or successful people and can be convinced something is true if a celebrity says it's true. If you are getting the hard sell from someone with a public reputation, consider carefully whether the sales pitch is valid – remember, they are being *paid* to promote products or causes.

Our parents

Our parents are one of the most influential sources in our lives. They are the first and primary source of influence in our lives. Their influence begins when we are infants and lasts forever. We are always connected to our parents and their influence will have lasting impact on our character.

Parents have a responsibility to raise children in a loving, safe, and positive atmosphere. Children will model the behavior of their parents, not necessarily their words. Children are constantly alert to what parents are doing.

Parents are normally the primary influencers of our self-image and identity. Unfortunately, they don't always do a good job. Thus, we must be alert to influences that are not good or appropriate. Just because a parent teaches or models some behavior, attitude, or habit, does not make it right. At some time every child must confirm or deny what has been modeled by family members.

Other people

Another influence can be friends and associates who are close to you and to whom you give a certain level of respect. But we should not rely on how other people view us to form our own self-image.

The approval of other people should never be a determining factor in evaluating your self-worth. Self-worth is not determined by a vote or by the number of people who like or dislike you. You cannot look to the praise of others to determine self-worth. If you live for the love and attention of others you will eventually be disappointed, and that time might come sooner rather than later.

People are flawed and have their own agendas.
It is neither logical nor reasonable to allow our self-worth to be determined by the wishes, thoughts, or desires of others, many of whom may be strangers. We cannot and should not live our lives based on what we believe someone else may think. Who knows what, how, or why

someone else may hold a certain view? And, why should we care? What validity should a stranger have on our self-image?

> *"The worst loneliness is to not be comfortable with yourself."*
> Mark Twain[23]

WHY IS SELF-IMAGE IMPORTANT?

It affects our health

If we have a distorted view of ourselves, many difficulties can occur: emotional problems, inappropriate feelings of self-worth, and low self-esteem. You can feel you simply don't measure up, which results in a lack of confidence and ultimately to many life disappointments. This can lead to eating disorders or use of alcohol and drugs.

The excessive pursuit of perfection, whether appearance, body-image, intellectual achievement, career advancement, or wealth, can lead to practices that have a negative impact on our lives. Balance is appropriate in all areas of our lives in order to maintain a healthy lifestyle.

It affects our relationships

Our self-image affects our relationships with others. If we have a poor self-image, we may have difficulty relating to others. We may feel inadequate around others, particularly people with good reputations and those with happy or more joy-filled lives.

Collecting "likes" on social media and posting pictures of your daily activities does not constitute a relationship or a social life. Activity on social media can take up significant time and accomplishes very little. If you have self-image problems, you may compare your social media activity with others and this causes the vicious cycle to begin, continue, and even escalate.

It can impact our spiritual life

Your self-image issues can affect whatever kind of relationship you have with your God. Trust and obedience to religious expectations can be difficult. You may even question God about your personal characteristics, situation, and relationships. You may begin to ask the question "Why?" about all facets of your life.

CONCLUSION

Our true identity is a critically important piece of our being. It will often determine what we say and do. Our words and actions will be directed by what we think of ourselves and what others think about us. It is often what we present to the world, particularly when we are with others or in the public eye.

Thus, negative or positive comments about our image or identity will have a significant impact on all portions of our life: private, public, business, and personal relationships. We listen to the fears or concerns of our hearts, the perceptions of others, and draw conclusions about our image and self-worth.

These conclusions can lead to positive or negative actions and reactions that will form the foundation of our lives. They determine whether we are comfortable with ourselves and dictate how we act and relate to others. Identity and self-image are so important that even the smallest negative or positive comment can have lasting impact on our life.

Because of the impact of identity in our lives we are often motivated to hide from others and even from ourselves because we are unsure, or have very little confidence in our abilities. Likewise if we have strong character and self-image we may demonstrate our abilities and skills to others simply because of our positive self-image.

Those with a positive self-identity will recognize that they are unique and that can be a strength. Weaknesses do not have to control our lives. We are valuable to others and ourselves, no matter what skills we possess, what we look like, or how we talk. We all have value and have a purpose in life. Regardless of your purpose, you are valuable.

"Never limit yourself to what you can't do, but to what you have the power to do with what you have."
Nadège Richards[24]

Wisdom to Action Challenge

Think about your self-image. Are you grounding it internally? Identify one way you can cultivate a more positive self-image this week, fostering genuine relationships and navigating life's challenges with confidence.

Chapter 6
Signs of a Distorted
Self-image

*"Be yourself – not your idea of what
you think somebody else's
idea of yourself should be."*
Henry David Thoreau[25]

*"The man who does not value himself,
cannot value anything or anyone."*
Ayn Rand[26]

GENERAL

In this chapter we are going to review many of the signs or behaviors that indicate you may have self-image issues. This outline is intended to give you an overview and understanding of the broad nature of our identity and how it can be shaped by ourselves, others, the world, and uncontrollable circumstances around us.

The primary focus of this chapter will be on the signs that indicate a struggle with self-image issues. First let's examine some general background that will help you better understand the signs and source of problems that might develop in your life.

What is normal?

An identity crisis is not necessarily normal but it should not be totally unexpected in a world of the internet, television, and social media. These technological capabilities allow others to have great impact on your self-image. They can both confirm the good and provide good advice and guidance, or they can totally mislead and damage your perception of self.

These forces can impact how you define yourself by guiding your thinking regarding your values, beliefs, and habits. They can also impact your hopes, desires, and interests. They may even shape your personality because they will guide you in determining what is good, bad, right, and wrong.

What is an identity crisis?

An identity crisis is a period of uncertainty and confusion in which a person's sense of identity becomes insecure, typically due to a change in their expected role in society.

I would say that if you are unsure of your purpose in life, or wonder why you exist at all, you are probably having an identity crisis. Such a crisis can impact your ability to perceive and understand the truth about what is right, wrong, good, or bad.

Gaining a sense of identity and maturity occurs in all of us. Becoming comfortable in your identity may be more difficult for some than others. It can lead to minor anxiety or ultimately to depression if issues are not resolved.

Identity issues can cause people to have difficulty with other characteristics that occur as one begins to mature.

Two of the most important are your level of self-esteem and self-control.

Low self-esteem

A distorted or very low feeling of self-worth (low self-esteem) occurs when you believe you have little value. This feeling can occur for many different reasons but generally happens because others (parents, friends, mentors, bosses, or teachers) tell you that you are worthless – or something to that effect.

If others judge or evaluate you harshly, the good and positive contributions you are making are often ignored and ultimately forgotten. In this case the truth about yourself becomes distorted, but the criticism sticks and it can be a battle to regain a correct understanding of the truth about yourself.

Low self-esteem generally does not develop as the result of one bad experience. It is usually the result of a number of negative experiences beginning in childhood and continuing through adulthood. The underlying cause might be abuse, bullying, isolation, physical failures, or academic failures.

These events can cause or encourage low self-esteem:

- Being punished or reprimanded harshly.
- Being ridiculed because of physical deformity.
- Being rejected by a friend or romantic interest.
- Being ignored by parents or friends.
- Being ridiculed or made fun of.
- Being a victim of abuse, crime, or addiction.
- Being a failure in some important undertaking (school, job, hobby, sport).

- Being criticized, corrected, or disciplined by someone in authority.
- Being a failure in business.
- Being divorced.

Seek solutions rather than obsess over the problems.

Low self-control

Poor self-control means you are not effective in controlling feelings, actions, or words and the result produces difficult situations or challenges that are hard to overcome. If taking positive action and persevering is difficult, you can find yourself in helpless situations. You may not speak up to defend yourself. You may not be able to control your temper. You may be unable to hold down a job.

These situations can often result in depression, arguments, or loss of jobs. You may feel you are unable to influence a bad situation and you feel helpless. You may be stuck in a situation and have no ability to extract yourself or improve the situation.

Distorted self-image

Again, if you have a distorted self-image, you will not see yourself in a way that is correct or accurate. Generally you think of yourself more negatively than is true.

TEN WARNING SIGNS

A person experiencing an identity crisis may be thinking about the following questions:

- What do I believe about the existence of God?
- Who am I?
- What is my life purpose?
- Why do I exist?
- What are my core values and moral standards?
- Do I have any real passions?

Everyone has questions about their existence at different times in their life journey. It becomes a crisis when those questions begin to cause physical, mental, or emotional stress that interferes in daily life situations. You become easily irritated, emotional, sad, or depressed.

Times of significant life change can be triggers for identity issues. Big changes can cause you to question your values, likes and dislikes, and even beliefs. You may begin to wonder where you fit into the greater scheme of life. These thoughts can result in reduced motivation for work, relationships, or other personal interests. They may even cause you to withdraw from family and other important personal relationships.

Following is a list of the most common signs that indicate you may be struggling with self-image or identity issues:

1. Circumstances dictate behavior

Your work, family environment, hobbies and interests dictate the way you act. You do not have a solid concept of self and your behavior changes to conform to your surroundings and situation.

2. Relationships impact you

You change your activities to match or conform to your friends and you are often oblivious to these changes. You may even change your likes and dislikes to match those of your friends or partner.

a. You frequently change your opinion
This may include such subjects as religious beliefs, music, books, fashion, or anything that would create conflict with a friend. Such change often swings back and forth on a weekly or monthly basis. You do this to please a friend or associate in order to find acceptance in their eyes.

b. You never talk about yourself
You are uncomfortable sharing about yourself or your views. You tend to change the subject if someone asks questions about you, your background, your beliefs, or even your likes and dislikes. You may respond to questions by asking the same question in return.

c. You have shallow relationships
You fear others will discover that you have self-image issues and then reject you or your friendship. Thus, the safe avenue is not to allow others to really know you. You may fear intimacy or sharing even normal personal issues.

3. You can't commit

You have difficulty feeling passionate about anything because that would seem to require a permanent commitment. Since you do not want to be tied down it is easy to avoid personal relationships. You may find it easy to move from one job to another frequently.

4. You don't trust yourself

If you make frequent mistakes in judgment, the result may be that you are afraid to trust your opinion about others or their behavior. Everything becomes unreliable, undependable, and trust is a very difficult character trait to establish.

5. You have low self-esteem

You feel you are inferior compared to others. You lack confidence in yourself. You are concerned about what others think of you and you find it difficult to ask for help because you see that as a sign of weakness.

You may tend to feel everyone is better than you and their skills and abilities are superior to yours. You may feel unattractive. The fear of being rejected by others drives your relationships.

6. You never feel comfortable

You never think you measure up to others. You feel inferior or not good enough to be involved with others or their activities. You are constantly concerned about how others see you. Since you are not comfortable, you will frequently put yourself down, describe yourself in unflattering terms, or even deny your abilities. You may wish you were invisible at social gatherings. This will cause you to be ill-at-ease and fearful of someone finding fault with you or your work. You are convinced that you or your work will be misunderstood.

7. You are obsessed about flaws being discovered

Since you feel unworthy you are constantly concerned someone will confirm that feeling and expose your flaws and insecurities. Therefore, you spend a great deal of time trying to hide your perceived flaws from others, even little inconsequential flaws. If and when a relationship has problems, you feel like a total failure. You spend a great deal of effort trying to protect yourself from being discovered. You're afraid to let people see "the real you."

8. Defeat is inevitable

When you experience loss, setbacks, negative feedback, stress, or hardship of any kind you are more than ready to blame yourself for the difficulties. You assume failure is inevitable. Thus, you are often defeated before you begin any undertaking.

9. You are indecisive

You have very little confidence and find it difficult to make decisions. You constantly seek the opinions of others. You may be fearful of negative consequences. You stall making decisions hoping you may not have to decide.

10. Your body-image is distorted

a. You are overly critical of your appearance.
You look in the mirror and see only flaws. It is absolutely normal to see or notice flaws you would like to fix, but if that holds your attention and causes you to feel unattractive, you need to rethink your understanding of being attractive.

b. You are ashamed of your appearance.
Shame is a strong and serious emotion. If you are ashamed of any part of your appearance or being, you need to change your perceptions and understanding. People can be cruel, often without thinking. You cannot allow others to cause you to feel shame. Their opinions may be coming from feelings about their own inadequacies, which you know nothing about.

c. Your self-worth is tied to your appearance.
Although this is a common symptom for many, it is an absolutely unreasonable conclusion. Your appearance has nothing to do with your self-worth. Others can give appearance value because it helps them sell something, but that has nothing to do with personal value and worth. Your self-worth is tied to your abilities, what you can do and produce, your goodness and kindness, and your contributions to people and society. It is a function of your contribution to the well-being of others and not tied to the size of your nose, lips, tummy, legs, feet, or anything else.

d. You spend excessive time on your appearance.
You should be fit. You should eat a good diet. It is helpful to dress nice. But fitness, weight, and body shape have no lasting and eternal value. Be more concerned about the

question of what you are doing with the skills, abilities, and gifts you possess.

e. Other related body-image issues.
Body image problems, symptoms, or signs will vary a great deal from one person to another. The following are some other typical signs that body image is a problem:

- Feeling unattractive.

- Maintaining unrealistic beauty standards.

- Prioritizing appearance over health.

- Determining self-worth based on appearance.

- Straining to achieve or maintain an unrealistic weight or clothing size.

- Never feeling satisfied with your appearance.

A distorted or incorrect view of your body will often remain with you for most of your life, unless you take intentional steps to correct the distorted view.
Lore Ferguson said the following in a Christianity Today article:

"When I think back to the times I felt most beautiful, most nourished, most comfortable with my body and its natural curves and inclinations, they were not the times I was most in control of those things, but the times I worried least about them. . . ."[27]

Beauty is not in the external things of life
but in the reflections of a soul well lived.

SUMMARY

The above ten signs are general in nature. There are other signs that are more specific and dramatic. You may exhibit lurid and promiscuous behavior. That will usually result in both romantic and personal relationship failures. If you are married, divorce is often a result. You may also find yourself hurting others through teasing, name-calling, or gossiping. Long-term relationships may be ignored and allowed to disintegrate or even disappear. Positive relationships may simply be ignored. Boredom and apathy my surround you.

On the work or career side of your life, strange decisions and conduct might be common. Intense feelings like anger or sadness may be exhibited. Pulling away from people and activities may occur. You may build walls that cause you to avoid conflict, problem-solving, or even normal contact with others.

Some of the worst signs might involve breaking and disregarding rules, limits, standards, and even laws. There may be disregard for acting right and following accepted standards of behavior.

Lastly, and one of the most devastating, is alcohol or drug addiction.

> *"Seeing, feeling, thinking, believing—*
> *these are the stages of how we*
> *change our style on the outside and*
> *our self-image on the inside."*
> Stacey London[28]

Wisdom to Action Challenge

Consider societal pressures. Are you conforming to external expectations? Identify one negative self-perception you can challenge this week, breaking free from self-doubt and creating a resilient self-image.

Chapter 7
Seasons of Life

"There is a time for everything,
and a season for every activity."
Solomon[29]

GENERAL

Identity and self-image are impacted greatly by the season of life you are experiencing. Are you a teenager trying to understand life? Are you entering your freshman year in college? Are you trying to land your first important job? Have you just been married? Has your first child just been born? Have you just experienced the death of a friend or family member?

What season of life are you in? Are there situations that exist in your life that seem to be the overriding forces? Is this season of your life something you expected and prepared for or is it a total shock to your system? It is one thing to know that we will all die one day. It is another to bury a child or a parent.

How are your life expectations, circumstances, and lifestyle impacting your identity? Are you in a positive season of life where you are:

- looking forward to what is around the next corner in your life?
- excited, energetic, diligent, hard working?
- creative?
- connected with others?
- growing and building your life and family?
- comfortable, mellow, satisfied, at peace?
- enjoying life?
- content and satisfied?

Or, are you in a negative season where you are:

- anxious, worried, or stressed?
- exhausted and tired?
- bored and apathetic?
- grieving?
- searching and not sure what you are looking for?
- hopeless and depressed?
- alone and lonely?
- sick?

Regardless of what circumstances might describe your life at the present time, it is important to recognize that there are different seasons in life and you are likely to experience most of them. These seasons will impact how you feel about yourself and life in general. They do not last forever so you should not think that life will not improve or that you are going to be permanently on top of the world. Youth will pass, the honeymoon will end, your health will improve, and your teenagers will begin to mature. If they don't mature, they will move out eventually and you won't have to deal with them on a daily basis anymore.

Life is a series of cycles that can seemingly last a long time or change overnight. Some of these cycles are good, some are bad, and some are just part of living life. To help you understand the nature of the changing cycles in your life we will briefly discuss some seasons of life that most people experience. Note how these seasons might impact your identity or self-image.

NORMAL SEASONS OF LIFE

1. The vigor and innocence of youth

When you are young you have little or no thought of death, disability, a greater purpose in life, or the amount of your retirement income. You have plenty of energy and you feel there is nothing you can't do. Unfortunately, the circumstances of life could damage or destroy that perspective and thinking, leaving you devastated. During this season of life we often give no thought to the future.

But reality will begin to take hold. Depending on how much you are focused on the romance of youth, your re-entry into the real world could be bumpy.

2. The difficulties of old age (infirmities and disabilities)

At the other end of the spectrum is the senior years, which may be filled with health problems. At their worst, they could destroy a good self-image. When you can't physically take care of yourself because of your health, it is very easy to lose hope and purpose. The indignities of someone else taking care of you are not easy to accept. If your health problems are associated with pain, your infirmities can be even more difficult to handle.

3. The excitement of young adulthood (seeking a career, finding true love, building a family, making a home)

This period of time can produce both positive and negative self-image issues. If you are having success with your job, your marriage, and good healthy children, life can be a parade. But if none of this is happening or if it is and it's all bad, that parade can feel like a funeral procession. The reality of life is that during this season you are probably having both wins and losses. Your identity may be undergoing serious change because major changes in life are occurring.

4. The pleasure of enjoying the fruit of your work, family, business, emerging wealth; a time of seeking new levels of satisfaction

Like young adulthood, this season of life could be great or because of disappointments and failure it could be terrible. Your self-image and identity may become solidified, and that could be either good or bad. Given this stage in life and the general age range you may be seeing self-image signs that are recurring. It may be more difficult to fix low self-esteem problems.

You now have more experience. This isn't your first battle with your self-image. You should now be far more capable of dealing with self-image issues. You not only have more experience, but you have resources available that you could not have afforded when you were younger. You understand far more about yourself and you are able to deal more effectively with the highs and the lows.

5. The difficulties of handling and living with failures, disappointments, losses

Regardless of when failures occur they are still very difficult to handle. This is true at any age and your ability to cope, understand the problem, and deal with it will often be a function of experience, maturity, and intentionality.

The patience and willpower needed to find healing, restoration, recovery, or transformation will depend on your ability to feel comfortable in your identity and having confidence in yourself to deal with difficulties.

6. Starting over, building new relationships, and finding new friends

The seasons in our lives when we are starting something new can be exciting and invigorating to the spirit. But they can also be times that are frightening or stressful. You can be challenged during these days. You may be thrown into new situations that you are not sure how to handle and your confidence can wane or be severely tested.

7. The days of sadness, loss, mourning, or leaving friends

Days of sadness, particularly days of grieving, can be very hard on your self-image. When you must leave good friends because one of you is moving, you may feel that your support system has just disappeared. When a friend, spouse, or family member dies you may grieve for an extended period of time.

These people have been contributing to your life and now they are gone. It is right and proper for us to grieve but we must also find replacements for the important part these

78

people played in our lives. Our focus on building up and ministering to self is very important in this season of life.

8. The days of great joy, happiness, satisfaction, contentment, celebration, and strong friendships

These are the wonderful seasons of our lives. We should enjoy them to the fullest extent possible. They will do wonders for our identity and self-image. Unfortunately they do not last forever. There is a season for every important event and not all of them will be permanent.

9. The days when leadership or bravery are required; when you must be outside your comfort zone

Bravery is not required for living outside your comfort zone, but it sure helps. Courage and bravery do not mean that you are not challenged or that you are not frightened and uncomfortable in a situation.

Courage means that you endure the discomfort and not let it stop you. It does not mean you feel no fear; it means that you proceed in spite of the fear and overcome it. Nothing is more satisfying to your self-image than overcoming the challenges we all face in life. The goal is to overcome the challenge, not allow the challenge to overcome you.

10. The days of solace, quietness, stillness, self-inspection, and taking stock

These are great periods in your life if you are an introvert. If you are an extrovert you may be bored and restless. Regardless of your inclinations, make these times useful and grow through meditation, self-examination, and planning. Recognize that these are times when your heart and spirit need quiet rejuvenation. If you are very busy and always in a hurry, these times may be necessary for your physical well-being. Go away for a few days and spend time thinking and recharging your batteries. Use these times to take stock of who and where you are.

11. A time to rebel against what is wrong or evil; supporting what is right, creating stress and conflict; a time to speak out and speak up

Conflict may be a dirty word in your life, but there are times when a cause or situation requires taking a stand. Good people cannot continually standby while evil is being practiced in our midst. There is a time when we may be required to take a stand, even if it will put great strain on our identity and self-image.

These times might be for something that is national in nature and will require government intervention. Or it may involve taking a stand against the abuse of a neighbor child. In either case your identity may be tested. Will you do what is right or needed in order to right a wrong?

12. A time to fix, restore, build, and repair

This season of life may follow the times described immediately above. It might involve fixing a relationship problem in your family or repairing your marriage. It could be that you need to rebuild a business. The subject could be any number of different challenges that you might have to face. You will be called on to do work and it could take a great deal of energy. Will you step up and do what is needed or will you shy away? This may require help from others. Don't be afraid to ask.

SUMMARY

Some of these descriptions of the different seasons in your life may be very real to you. In fact you may have scars that are still healing. Or you may remember or be in the midst of a really wonderful season in your life.

The important understanding is that your self-image and identity will be impacted by these seasons. And the season, good or bad, may be totally out of your control. So be prepared to deal with life when it happens to you. You will be shaped by these seasons and your goal should be to learn, grow, and mature from these life experiences.

You must engage life and use good and bad seasons to make yourself into the very best you can be. Don't allow the seasons to shape you into someone you are not or don't want to be. Grow and mature in the seasons. Use them to strengthen your character and improve your self-esteem. Don't allow them to pull you down or lower your self-image. Use these seasons to acquire strength and stature. Remember, you can often learn more from failure and disappointment than from success and satisfaction.

"Be faithful to that which exists within yourself."
Andre Gide[30]

```
┌─────────────────────────────────────────────┐
│  ┌───────────────────────────────────────┐  │
│  │       Wisdom to Action Challenge       │  │
│  └───────────────────────────────────────┘  │
│  ┌───────────────────────────────────────┐  │
│  │  Reflect on the current season of your │  │
│  │  life. How can you maintain a positive  │  │
│  │  core identity despite challenges?      │  │
│  │  Identify one action you can take this  │  │
│  │  week to nurture your values,           │  │
│  │  abilities, and accomplishments.        │  │
│  └───────────────────────────────────────┘  │
└─────────────────────────────────────────────┘
```

Chapter 8
How to Improve Your Self-image

*"Don't let mental blocks control you.
Set yourself free. Confront your fear and turn
the mental blocks into building blocks."*
Dr. Roopleen[31]

GENERAL

Having a positive identity and self-image will help you live a better life, overcome obstacles, and give you the strength and courage to accomplish goals and objectives. It will help you identify and maintain core values that will support high moral standards.

If you have a negative self-image or if you are not sure who you are and what purpose you have in life, you will generally have an uphill battle in achieving the person you want to be. A poor or weak self-image can be improved. You can do many things to develop a strong identity.

But don't dwell or spend hours and days worrying about your image or identity. Don't become obsessed with the subject. Understand the difference between normal activities and efforts to improve or build a good self-image.

If you have body-image issues your physical appearance can be particularly troublesome because it can cause:

- distress in social or occupational settings
- eating disorders
- depression
- anxiety
- shame

These difficulties can cause or create even more serious physical or emotional disorders. The issues are more likely to get worse than to disappear or become insignificant, so they must be addressed not ignored.

Building or fixing your self-image will take effort, perseverance, and intentionality. One of the biggest hurdles in overcoming identity issues is knowing whether there really is a problem or if, in fact, there is no problem at all. Our emotions and feelings in the area of identity and self-image can make it difficult to cultivate good habits and behaviors that lead to improved self-image.

Taking one or more of the actions described in the following pages will help you build a positive self-image. Doing one or more of these actions does not mean that you will immediately fix a problem. Long- term and permanent success will often require time. But success can be achieved.

HOW TO OVERCOME PROBLEMS

Fortunately, there are many things you can do to improve your self-image. It is important to understand that you are not alone in feeling this way and that there is hope in all seasons of life. Following are a number of actions to take that will help you overcome or improve particular issues.

1. You must accept yourself

This is the first and probably the most import decision. And, it truly is a decision. It's a choice that you make. Your life includes all your strengths, weaknesses, flaws, skills, etc. This does not mean that you accept or will always be burdened with particular flaws or weaknesses. Accept weaknesses for what they are and determine if they are important enough to change or improve.

Understand the thoughts and feelings you have about your image and identity. It is natural to have thoughts and feeling about yourself. Be aware of your inner feelings and concerns. Be particularly aware of negative or dangerous thoughts. Recognize anxiety that is the result of low self-esteem.

In some cases you may want to talk with family, friends, or simply take intentional actions to think positive thoughts. Try to be compassionate toward your own feelings and thoughts. Everyone, no matter what the situation, needs and deserves compassion. Are you putting yourself down and lacking confidence in yourself? If so, you may have self-image issues that need to be addressed.

2. Believe you can improve

This is similar to accepting yourself, but is more action oriented. Make the decision that you can change, build, and improve on any self-image issues that are holding you down. Nothing beats a positive attitude when it comes to restoration or transformation.

3. Kill the negative thoughts

Negative self-talk is one of the most debilitating habits that can prevent making improvements in your life. Constantly tell yourself that you can rather than believe that you can't. Think positively and when you begin negative self-talk, counteract it with affirmations about yourself.

If you regularly dwell on negatives in your life, create a pattern of positive responses that will move your focus away from negative thoughts to positive thoughts. Prepare specific responses to negative thoughts.

4. Adjust your expectations

Change your expectations if they are unreasonable or do not fit with your personality, skills, or goals. But don't set your goals and objectives at unreasonable levels. We can assure you that you will never be perfect. Your goal is not perfection: it is improvement. Any degree of improvement is good. If you make progress every day, no matter how little, real improvement will soon be evident.

Focus on doing your best and know that your best will be good enough. Adjust your timeframe expectations if change is taking longer than you projected. There is nothing wrong with slow positive improvement. What is wrong is giving up, accepting the "inevitable," or believing that you are stuck in this place forever. You will only be stuck if you allow yourself to be stuck.

5. Rely on your strengths

Every person has a unique set of strengths and skills. Use your skills and strengths to improve your condition. Even small improvements will help you gain confidence. Simply hoping that weaknesses will improve so that you can make progress is usually a fool's journey.

Using your strengths will assure progress. Progress creates confidence. Confidence is the foundation of self-image. As your confidence builds you will experience a more positive self-image. Therefore, know your strengths, build on them, and use them wisely to define, establish, and build your real identity.

6. You are unique

Knowing and using what makes you unique will result in significant improvement in identity and self-image. You may have certain skills, talents, or abilities that set you apart. For example: voice, athletic skill, intelligence, computer savvy, or having a friendly personality add up to unique personal characteristics.

Embrace these abilities no matter how small you think they may be. When you celebrate them, others will as well. Use your special traits to your advantage. Don't try to be like everyone else. It is your uniqueness that will draw you to others and to other activities.

7. Be good and kind

You can't beat acting rightly. Be friendly, not standoffish. Kindness and goodness can never be replaced. If you are inherently good and exhibit kindness to all those around you, people will be drawn to your. I heard someone say, "It costs nothing to be kind. Why would you choose to be ugly and mean?" Small acts of kindness often have far greater value to a recipient because they are personal in nature.

One of the most effective ways to feel good about yourself is to do deeds of mercy and compassion. Helping others will do amazing things for your mental and emotional health. Your brain can even release beneficial chemicals into your system when you help others.

Feeling good about yourself tends to cause body-image issues to fade into the background. Have you ever put your hand on someone's shoulder or shared a hug with one who needed comfort? They will remember your gesture even without words.

8. Be grateful

The value of being grateful and living a life of gratitude is similar to being good and kind. There is nothing more noticeable to others than one who is grateful for life: good times, bad times, or whatever. They find the good things in any situation. Be thankful and everyone will notice. Your identity will reflect the gratitude you display.

Some people who want to improve their gratitude will create lists of what they are grateful for. The result is that the focus of their life is placed on the positive, not the negative. A gratitude list will often result in thanking people for their contribution to your life. People will respond to positive words and situations much better than if the situation is negative. Tell others how much you appreciate them.

Yes, you may have difficulties and problems, but don't let the negative overshadow the positive. Be positive! Put negative thoughts and ingratitude out of your mind. You can be grateful for your health, your family, your friends, your job, or your co-workers. Anything that is positive in your life can be a reason for gratitude. Be thankful for the help or presence of a friend. Find ways to encourage others for how they contribute to your life.

9. Stop the comparisons

Comparing yourself to others or other situations is never a worthwhile experience or process. Everybody walks his own life journey and whether yours is better or worse than someone else's will have very little immediate or eternal purpose.

The circumstances of others may or may not make them happy or give them satisfaction. You have heard the saying about the grass being greener on the other side of the fence. Looks can be deceiving. You cannot know the real situation when you observe from a distance.

The primary person worthy of your time is yourself! You cannot be your best for others if are not good to yourself. Don't neglect your own needs. Make yourself the priority but never ignore the real needs of others.

It is good to take inspiration from others but only to encourage yourself to grow and improve. Comparisons in general are not productive because everyone is unique. Other people are always going to have certain characteristics that are better than you. Frankly, they also have some that may be a whole lot worse. That is the nature of life. The skills or strengths of others exist to benefit them, not you. Take more time to determine your real needs rather than covet the strengths of another.

10. Pursue self-help and personal growth

Your first investment must be in yourself. Personal growth activities can lead to significant life improvement. As you grow in understanding and skills, your confidence will rise and the inevitable result is a better self-image. There are many possibilities and sources for gaining personal growth: books (like this one), webinars, internet courses, workshops, podcasts, or seminars.

For serious problems or when you want personal one-on-one guidance you can hire counselors or therapists.

11. Set boundaries and have rules

Avoid the obvious pitfalls by establishing rules and boundaries relating to areas where you need help and want to concentrate. Stay away from situations that will lead you into trouble.

Don't spend time with people who create problems for you. The drug addict must drop all associations with former friends with whom he did drugs. It is important to surround yourself with friends and associates who are positive and encouraging.

Avoid all negative influences that would cause you grief. Avoid certain books and magazines. Avoid certain podcasts. Get off social media with those people who cause you problems and are not sympathetic to your needs. Change the people, activities, or situations that tend to poison or negatively influence your mind.

12. Engage in self-care

First and foremost, take care of yourself. Spend time with people who are positive and care about you. Do things that you enjoy and that lift you up and bring you peace. If your present friends and associates don't share your values and interests, find people who do.

Self-care is not necessarily expensive or time-consuming. It can be simple little pleasures that bring you joy, happiness, or peace. It can be as simple as sitting on the porch watching the world go by. But it can be going to the mountains skiing alone because no one in your present crowd enjoys skiing. See further suggestions in chapters 11A and 11B for self-care or self-love.

13. Help others

We believe one of the broad purposes of man is to help those in need. Being kind and compassionate to those with special needs can be very rewarding. If you feel down, sad, or depressed, do something good for somebody. Many people need encouragement today.

How could you pay it forward? What could you do to lift the spirits of another? How could you encourage a friend that is going through a bad time? How could you help someone grieve? How could you help someone who is home-bound? What special skills do you have that could be a blessing to others? Rather than focusing on yourself, focus on how you can help and benefit others.

14. Slow down

Change and improvement in self-image can take time. It will not occur overnight. Take reasonable steps to improve or build your identity. Don't bite off more than you can chew. Attack the small parts of your self-image problem first in order to determine reasonable expectations. Don't set yourself up for failure because you try to do too much.

15. Stop negative self-talk

Don't be your worst enemy by telling yourself that you don't deserve something. Everyone has flaws. Replace any negative thoughts about yourself with positive ones. Overcome the tendency to think negative thoughts.

16. Appreciate yourself

Think about what you are good at. What makes you unique and interesting? Before you go to sleep at night think about one thing that makes you special. Remember, there is nothing wrong with being average. Not everyone is a celebrity, CEO, star athlete, or social media influencer.

Appreciate yourself for who you are and don't agonize over who you wish you were. Are there areas of our lives you might want to improve? Certainly! But don't be overly focused on the wish list. Be satisfied and confident in the "I am" list.

17. Eat right

This suggestion might seem a bit obvious but it is a fundamental truth. Many of us neglect our health, particularly when it comes to eating right. Eat the right food and your body will love you. If your self-image is a bit distorted, that condition can be enhanced by the food you eat and whatever else you may put in your body. If you put garbage into your body, that's what you are going to get back. Eat right, sleep right, and drink right. Don't forget the exercise.

Don't limit yourself to a life without treats. If you want to treat yourself, then do it. You will feel amazing and appreciative, as long as those treats aren't daily.

18. Participate in activities that you love (music, arts, public service, or sports)

Do what you enjoy. Have fun and enjoy life. Take part in some form of music, arts, or sports. Engage in hobbies and activities that you enjoy. If you are sitting at home with negative self-talk it is very easy to fall into a state where you have a negative self-image. When you are active and doing things you enjoy those negative thoughts will be replaced by positive thoughts.

19. Self-examination

If you are investigating feelings about yourself, examine the activities and hobbies that you have a passion for. Have your interests changed? Self-examination is a good way to get in touch with yourself again. Remember that you are not one-dimensional. You have many aspects to your life. Build on your strengths and bring them to bear on the different aspects of your life. This will help you strengthen your personal ability and encourage self-care.

Look within to identify the qualities and characteristics that define you and make you feel either good or bad. What produces sadness in your life? What are the core values that are the foundation of your life? How do your interests, passions, and hobbies support your core values?

What are your life goals? What do you want to accomplish? What makes you happy, sad, excited, or nervous? Is there a personal need that you are not fulfilling? Satisfying a need in life can be very uplifting.

20. Get help

Friends and family can be a very helpful in your quest for change. Get feedback from people you trust. There are many types of support groups available that will provide help if you have identity issues. Friends, family, social groups, religious groups, team sports groups, and professional support groups can all be great places to find support you may need. Professional help is always available if you think it is needed. If you suffer from depression, professional help can often be a godsend.

However, not everyone will care about your image or identity. Not everyone wants to be your friend. You want associates who support you, encourage you, guide you, lift you up, and boost your ego. You do not want friends and associates that drain the life out of you.

Who do you turn to when trouble occurs, disappointments mount, or life seems out of control? If your life is really falling apart it might be your immediate family or very close friends.

When the unexpected occurs, like the loss of a job, serious accident, divorce, serious illness, or death of a child, you need support. Experiencing one of these situations will quickly teach you that friends and good relationships are invaluable in life. It is very difficult to travel through the devastating experiences of life without people and relationships that you can depend on.

Some may believe that if they have resources like wealth and success they can weather anything that comes their way. They are usually wrong because wealth cannot love you, sit with you, talk with you, encourage you. Only true friends will do that.

21. Challenge negative stories

Don't allow negative thoughts, feeling, and stories about yourself to gain momentum in your heart or mind. Even when such thoughts are mostly true, don't spend time thinking or dwelling on negative experiences. Don't judge yourself, even if you did something that you wish you could undo. Allow yourself to make mistakes and be wrong. Nobody gets through life without wishing they had done something differently. You are human and you, your friends, and your enemies will all make mistakes.

Positive self-talk is a must whenever we do something wrong or make unwise decisions. Fix the situation as best you can and encourage yourself to be better in the future. Focus on the positive aspects of the situation rather than the negative. And, don't cast blame.

22. Deal with mistakes

The important thing is what you do about the mistakes you make in life. Do you seek forgiveness? Do you apologize? Do you try to correct or fix the situation? Learn from the experience and use it as a catalyst to improved performance and a better self-image.

We all make mistakes. Make sure you understand that mistakes can be fixed. Probably the worse course of action is to do nothing. Develop the strength to address issues and problems that cause hurt to others or yourself.

23. Practice forgiveness

No matter what the problem or the offense, forgive yourself and forgive others. Do it for yourself! There is nothing more senseless than carrying the burden of lack of forgiveness when a few well-chosen words can relieve your pain or trauma. If your past behavior was hurtful to you or others, make it right.

TIPS YOU COULD USE

a. Underline, circle, or highlight the tips, ideas, or concepts above that you think would make the most impact if you implemented them in your life. You will revisit these choices at the end of the book in the planning section.

b. There may be other ideas that you think could improve your self-image. Write them below:

_____

_____

_____

_____

_____

_____

"Whenever a negative thought concerning your personal power comes to mind, deliberately voice a positive thought to cancel it out."
Norman Vincent Peale[32]

Wisdom to Action Challenge

Evaluate your self-worth. Are you basing it on external factors? Identify one way you can define your self-worth internally this week, cultivating a stable identity and avoiding social comparison.

Chapter 9
Body-Image Issues

*"The surest way to lose your self-worth
is by trying to find it through the eyes of others."*
Becca Lee[33]

*"Total, unconditional acceptance of yourself
is the first step in building a positive self-image."*
Nido R Qubein[34]

Anyone can have body-image issues, even the most in-shape person. Body-image issues can occur at any time in life. Not surprisingly, pregnant women often suffer with their body-image and sometimes for months after child birth until they get their normal body back.

Body-images issues aren't a simple problem because they can have any number of underlying causes. It is not easy knowing the cause unless it is the obvious result of pregnancy, disability, or other obvious visual clues. The most common causes are:

- Body weight, shape, or height outside the accepted norms.
- Teasing and bullying, often experienced at a young age.

- Verbal abuse about appearance.
- Ugly messages and comments in social media.
- Shunning by family, classmates, friends, or co-workers.

Sometimes there is no obvious reason at all, but simply ideas and concepts imposed by society. This can often be the most difficult to deal with because there is no specific reason to address and fix.

BODY-IMAGE ISSUES

If you struggle with body-image issues, don't expect to conquer them overnight. It will normally take some effort and continuing attention. If you feel your body appearance is not attractive, then prepare for a reasonable time to overcome those feelings and self-doubt.

Most of the general suggestions listed in the previous chapter can be used to improve your feelings about your body. Specifically consider the following suggestions to help overcome body-image issues and build a better and more accurate perception of your physical appearance.

1. Recognize your personal situation

How much of your perceptions are the result of negative comments you heard as a youth or teenager? Mean comments could have come from friends, people in authority, or even family. Anyone can be unkind anytime, particularly if they want to hurt or stifle someone else.

How much negative talk made its way to your heart and mind? Understand it's just a matter of replacing the negative with the positive and the truth.

2. What wrong beliefs have you adopted?

You may have adopted some invalid and limiting beliefs about yourself without really evaluating what you were thinking. If you adopted invalid beliefs or opinions then it is easy to explain away failures based on those beliefs. Evaluate the stories you are telling yourself and determine whether they are true or false.

Develop a new and true story line. Replace the false and negative narrative. Don't worry about convincing others of your new story. The only one who must believe it is you. Others will follow your lead.

3. Focus on your strengths

You have gifts, talents, skills, and unique capabilities. Focus on your strengths. We touched on this subject in #5 in the previous chapter.

4. Ditch the diet and adopt a new eating lifestyle

Diets will end and so will your hopes of success. If you want to change your eating habits, then you need a lifestyle change. Diets only work for a short period of time and then any weight you may have lost will make a return visit. Short-term diets often contribute to anxiety because you know it is not going to be a real change. The only real solution is permanently changing your eating habits.

5. Positive self-talk

Positive self-talk means that we stop the negative self-talk (see #15 in previous chapter). Whenever negative thoughts raise their ugly messages, counter them with a new story and positive self-talk. Position and condition your brain to switch to your new story whenever you begin to have thoughts about a negative self-image.

6. Reduce your time on social media

People who sell beauty products don't want you to feel good about yourself. Influencers and sales people want to sell you something that "will change your life." Have you ever noticed that the people these influencers use as examples are already attractive in real life? No one is ever compared to everyday normal people.

Take a break from social media or avoid it altogether. Social media has no real value to the user unless they are keeping in touch with family and friends. Block the haters and trolls. Don't follow or pay any attention to people who want to create chaos. Anyone who makes you feel bad about yourself has no reason to be in your life.

Blocking or ignoring people in your social circle can sometimes be very difficult. Co-workers and family can be particularly troublesome. Set appropriate boundaries. Let the offender know your limits. Know in advance what you are going to say when it is necessary to respond.

Don't expect people to change unless you tell them they crossed a line. It doesn't require a long explanation. Just tell them how you feel. If they do not change their talk, reduce your exposure to them. On social media you can actually block them. In real life, it may be more difficult to avoid them.

7. Reduce impact of other health issues

Body-image issues may be the result of physical ailments. For example you might suffer from certain mood disorders, muscle problems, sexual dysfunction, self-harming tendencies, eating disorders, alcohol abuse, drug abuse, or other harmful behaviors. Take whatever steps necessary to face and resolve these issues.

PREGNANCY

If you deal with self-image issues, pregnancy may be a particularly difficult time for you. Pregnancy causes significant changes in a woman's body: weight gain, swelling, complexion problems, stretch marks, etc. It is not unexpected that these changes will cause self-image issues, even for women who don't ordinarily have body-image questions.

Your body is a fantastic mechanism for birthing a new life. Many find the pregnant form pleasing and celebrate the miracle that is taking place. Decide to be one of those people. Don't make yourself an invalid during pregnancy unless you have real health issues. Try to do all the normal things, but tone it down a bit, particularly in the latter stages of your pregnancy.

I ove yourself and how you look. Self-care demands that you love yourself and your body during this exciting time. Your body is exploding with joy. Enjoy the ride. Happiness and joy begin with accepting your condition and all the crazy things that will happen. Feel secure in the realization that these changes are temporary.

During this time emotional stability is often stretched to the breaking point. These body changes are not easy to deal with and can affect mental and emotional stability. Women who are normally calm may exhibit strong aggressive character traits while they are pregnant.

So, what to do? Because of the unique situation of pregnancy the poor body-image feelings are often short term. One could adopt some or all of the following in order to reduce the stress of pregnancy and the related body-image issues:

- Follow all good health recommendations your doctor gives you.

- Focus on the child being born. The body is making new life and you have little control over what the body is doing and how it will look.

- Don't hide your feelings. Tell others how you are feeling.

- A massage will often relieve stress and discomfort.

- Intellectually know what your body is doing and what to expect.

- Recognize that hormonal imbalances can occur. Share such feelings with your doctor.

- Be aware that post-partum depression is a real medical issue. Don't ignore it or try to treat yourself. See your doctor if feelings of sadness or depression linger.

TIPS YOU COULD USE

a. Underline, circle, or highlight the tips, ideas, or concepts above that you think would make the most impact if you implemented them in your life. You will revisit these choices at the end of the book in the planning section.

b. There may be other ideas that you think could improve your self-image. Write them below:

_____

_____

_____

_____

"I am my own experiment.
I am my own work of art."
Madonna[35]

Wisdom to Action Challenge

Think about societal standards. Are you prioritizing your health over external ideals? Identify one step you can take this week to cultivate self-acceptance, challenging negative self-talk and reducing exposure to harmful media.

Chapter 10
Low Self-Esteem

"Self-esteem is like a battery.
When the battery is charged,
the person is positive;
when the battery is low,
the individual is negative."
Lilly Harry[36]

GENERAL

Low self-esteem can impact nearly every phase of your life. If you think you are worthless, then you will act as if you are worthless, and you then become worthless. It's a self-fulfilling prophecy.

You will not seek relationships because you don't feel good about yourself and you fear being honest or intimate with someone else. Life in general is difficult because you have very low expectations and feel you are not deserving of good outcomes. Life can become lonely and challenging.

Your social life may be so hard for you to maintain that you simply give up.

If your confidence is low it will be hard to stand out in the job market. Employers are looking for strong, assertive people with self-confidence and you don't have that mind-set. When you do find a job, you may find it difficult to hold on to it because you may tend to minimize your contributions to the work load.

Seeking a normal education or engaging in ongoing education after high school or college may be challenging as well. It will be easy to think, "What's the use?"

If you begin to care less about life and your well-being, your health can suffer.

And, finally, when nothing is working out well, your general level of satisfaction and contentment will disappear. You will not find joy in life. You may conclude that you must live with this distorted view of yourself and that there is no escape. You may give up entirely.

The good news is that all these negative feeling can be reversed if you are willing.

IMPACT OF LOW SELF-ESTEEM

What are the events or factors in your life that are impacting how you feel about yourself? What messages are recurring in your mind that are pulling you down and holding you back? What is preventing your success, freedom, growth, independence, or joy?

Do you feel in control of your destiny or do you feel trapped? What forces or factors are making you feel like a prisoner? Are there parts of your life in which you feel you have no control? If you suffer from low self-esteem you may feel inadequate or ineffective in any number of areas. Low self-esteem will often hinder achievement of goals and impact many phases of life, not just one. Thus, you may have problems in parenting, job performance, learning and education, and relationships. These issues can lead to addictions, failed marriages, poor health, loss of jobs, or poor family relationships.

"Believe in yourself up here and it
will make you stronger than
you could ever imagine."
Sarah Dessen[37]

1. Impact in children

Low self-esteem in children can be serious because it leads to confidence issues and feelings of worthlessness. These feelings can stay with an individual all his life if not reversed. A child with low self-esteem may have difficulty in school and in making friends. Risky behavior and poor decisions are often common in children with low self-esteem.

2. Impact in teens

Teens who have low self-esteem may be insecure and be continually searching on how to fit into their environment. They may participate in questionable or risky behaviors. Eating disorders and experimentation with drugs can become a particular problem as teens try to cope.

3. Impact in adult

Adults with low self-esteem will experience negative feelings of worth and abilities. Relationships and successful careers may be very difficult. Depression, anxiety, and low energy are typical symptoms.

4. Impact in general

Relationships and careers are often difficult because of low self-esteem. General peace and contentment will suffer. Marriages may be at risk. Low self-esteem can lead to depression and anxiety problems. Stressful situations can be particularly difficult.

Social life can be challenging because confidence is lacking. It is common for those with self-esteem problems to suffer from feelings of inferiority and have only superficial relationships with friends and associates. This may cause one to pull away from social situations and even become a loner, or at a minimum avoid social situations.

5. Impact on career or education

Those who suffer from low self-esteem may find it difficult to maintain a job. Lack of confidence, poor interpersonal relationships, and feelings of incompetence can cause problems in all phases of life. People who suffer from low self-esteem may have problems in school because they believe their intelligence is not high enough and they tend to avoid taking on challenges for fear of failing.

6. Impact on health

Those who struggle with low self-esteem may neglect their physical well-being. They might choose to skip meals, avoid fitness work outs, and not get adequate sleep. They might even start to neglect personal hygiene.

Because they are not pleased with their image or identity they may slide into questionable activities. This might include alcohol, drugs, or sexual immorality.

7. Impact on emotional and mental health

Addictions, emotional instability, and mental stress can lead to other serious health issues. People may engage in dangerous behavior in an attempt to escape the feelings of negative self-worth. Things can even get to a point that they might consider suicide.

8. Impact on general well-being

People with low self-esteem may struggle to be happy, content, and lead normal lives because nothing is fulfilling. Because they feel they are not good enough and don't deserve a good life they may simply shut down and not try. If they feel their lives will never improve and nobody cares, life can be very difficult.

People with low self-esteem will tend to be at higher risk for poor general health because negative feelings will impact a good diet and normal exercise, and can lead to various other illnesses that could be prevented by a normal healthy lifestyle.

SUMMARY – CONCLUSION

That's the bad news. And it's real. But it does not have to be permanent and hold you down forever. Although you may not be perfect, that is not a "death sentence." Everyone, and we mean everyone, has flaws, often far more than onlookers recognize. The difference is those who appear to have it all together have found ways to deal with or hide their flaws so that the flaws do not significantly impact their life.

You and I just don't see much evidence of problems in those we see as successful people. Usually successful people have maximized their strengths and minimized their weaknesses. They have found ways to minimize the impact of their flaws.

If you are shy and poor at public speaking you should probably not consider a career in politics. You are much more likely to be successful at jobs requiring research, speech-writing for others, or personal accounting.

"At every given moment we are absolutely perfect for what is required for our journey."
Steve Maraboli[38]

Wisdom to Action Challenge

Consider negative beliefs. Are you recognizing your inherent value? Identify one positive affirmation you can repeat daily this week, challenging negative thought patterns and prioritizing internal validation.

Chapter 11A
Solution: Self-love

"You yourself, as much as anybody
in the entire universe, deserve
your love and affection."
Buddha[39]

"Believe in yourself!
Have faith in your abilities!
Without a humble but reasonable
confidence in your own powers
you cannot be successful or happy."
Norman Vincent Peale[40]

WHAT IS SELF-LOVE?

There is much said about self-love in today's culture. It sounds great, but what does it really mean? Can we really change our self-image and identity to make a difference?

Self-love includes how you think about yourself, how you treat yourself, and your feelings and emotions about yourself. Self-love dictates that you treat yourself right, talk to yourself right, and think about yourself right. You have a positive view of yourself that does not change when difficulties emerge.

Self-love means that you respect yourself and treat yourself accordingly. You treat yourself with the kindness and goodness of a loving parent or friend who understands you. You consider yourself of infinite worth and live, work, and play with a positive perception of yourself. When you make a mistake, you know that it can be fixed.

Does this mean that you are always totally happy and content? Of course not! Everyone experiences difficulties, but those don't change the basic way you think about yourself and how you treat yourself. Anyone has the right to be upset with himself for mistakes or disappointments. But that does not really impact the love one has for self.

This might be illustrated by how one feels about a child who makes a mistake or even a huge error in judgment. The parent may discipline the child, but the love for the child does not change. The parent will forgive the child for the lapse in judgment but that does not mean that the error is erased or should be repeated.

Self-love is like this. The love is not impacted by the daily ups and downs of living life. It is unconditional in all seasons of life.

The following are examples of what self-love might look like In action.

1. Asking for help when needed. Recognize that you can't do everything yourself.
2. Saying and thinking positive things about yourself.
3. Forgiving yourself and not holding grudges.

4. Not allowing others to take advantage of you.
5. Prioritizing yourself and your health.
6. Holding yourself accountable and taking responsibility for your words and actions.
7. Giving yourself rewards to celebrate victories.
8. Valuing your feelings, emotions, and thoughts.
9. Living in accordance with your core values.
10. Pursuing your interests, passions, hobbies, and goals: those things that you desire.

Sometimes if we have done something awful or hurtful, we might wonder if self-love is appropriate. It can be hard to even consider forgiving yourself and moving on if the consequences are serious. The key is to separate the poor actions or results from the underlying tendencies and influences of the human condition. You can love yourself and not love your actions or the result you caused.

TIPS YOU COULD USE

a. Underline, circle, or highlight the tips, ideas, or concepts above that you think would make the most impact if you implemented them in your life. You will revisit these choices at the end of the book in the planning section.

b. There may be other ideas that you think could improve your self-image. Write them below:

_____

_____

_____

_____

WHY SELF-LOVE?

Utilize your strengths, positive personality traits, and unique skills. Focus on what you do well and not on your weaknesses. Why would you try to fix a car if you know nothing about gas engines? Don't speak to large crowds if you are terrified of public speaking. Do the things you are good at.

There is only one of you, so be good to yourself. Once others realize you are comfortable with your identity, they will also be comfortable with you. Don't compare yourself with people you see on TV, the internet, or in magazines. You are unique and special. Appreciate yourself.

The importance of self-love cannot be overstated. Treating oneself with care and compassion requires the same actions and responses that you would utilize with a true friend. For some of you this may be very easy because you saw it modeled by family or friends. However, not everyone has the experience and teaching of a mentor or parent to guide them in self-image issues.

If you grew up in a very critical atmosphere with little tolerance, you might find it difficult to avoid self-criticism. If your foundation for love and compassion is lacking it might take some work and practice to make good self-love decisions.

Self-love allows one to grow in the midst of difficulties and pursue goals that others will give up on because they have no foundation in practicing self-care.

Many of the self-image issues that cause people to struggle are really born in an atmosphere where self-love was not taught, practiced, experienced, or celebrated. If self-love is missing it will be replaced by insecurities, worry, anxiety, and stress.

Conversely, if self-love exists there will be confidence, joy, satisfaction, and ultimately contentment. Our self-image and identity impacts all aspects of our lives and activities. We must believe that we have inherent value no matter who we are, no matter where we came from, and no matter what we look like.

To determine some understanding of your level of self-love, think about the following questions:

- Do you believe that you determine your own self-worth? Or do you believe other people determine your self-worth?

- When you make a mistake, do you forgive yourself and move on? Or do you blame and shame yourself?

- Do you feel guilty when you treat yourself well?

Does your self-love tank ever run dry? Does the weight of all the challenges in life seem to descend on you all at once? Do you feel exhausted trying to protect yourself?

If this is where you are today, you may be feeling vulnerable, frustrated, or emotionally drained. These are all fears and distortions we can feel when times are particularly stressful.

PRACTICING SELF-LOVE

Self-love (any act of self-care) has nothing to do with your relationship to others. Self-care does not mean that you are better or worse than anyone else. It is simply treating yourself with the respect you naturally deserve. You are making no statement relative to anyone else when you treat yourself well.

Acts of self-love do not seek validation from others. Someone with a true sense of self-love and self-care knows how truly distant they are from perfection. This same sense of self will help you have a sense of compassion for others. It is easier to be kind to others when you understand how challenging it can be to maintain a positive self-identity.

It might sound like it should be easy to be good to yourself. That's not always the case! If what you need to do is hard for you, then you might put it off and never get around to doing it. You might be thinking:

- I'll do this next week. I have more important things to work on now.
- Taking care of me seems a little selfish.
- This is going to be difficult.
- I don't think this is going to work.
- I don't think I can do this.
- This friendship is not good but it's better than nothing.
- I have not "eaten healthy" for years and nothing bad has happened to me.

It's normal not to want to commit to self-love or any other significant change in your life. The reality is that self-love does not take a lot of time or effort. It simply takes intentionality.

You can start slowly and work at your own pace. You do not need to tackle the entire problem at once. Do one thing per day or one significant thing per week. Recording you challenges and successes is often very helpful. Keep a journal of your experiences as you implement change in your life.

Self-love can become second nature if you are determined. This is a skill which can be practiced and honed. You can become very good at it. The keys are patience and perseverance. Make a plan and stick to it.

TIPS YOU COULD USE

a. Underline, circle, or highlight the tips, ideas, or concepts above that you think would make the most impact if you implemented them in your life. You will revisit these choices at the end of the book in the planning section.

b. There may be other ideas that you think could improve your self-image. Write them below:

_____

_____

_____

_____

*"I never loved another person
the way I loved myself."*
Mae West[41]

Wisdom to Action Challenge

Reflect on self-worth. Are you rejecting societal pressures?
Identify one action you can take this week to cultivate self-love,
grounding your identity in character and personal growth.

Chapter 11B
Self-Love Tips

"You've been criticizing yourself for years and it hasn't worked. Try approving of yourself and see what happens."
Louise Hay[42]

GENERAL

In the last chapter we discussed the reasons self-love is beneficial and included a list of acts that you might perform in order to treat yourself better. This chapter will focus on the practical aspects of self-care and self-love.

We will examine acts that you can do to strengthen your self-image, provide a sense of security, and give you steps for building a strong foundation for your identity. That foundation is something you can build and maintain yourself. You don't necessarily need outside help. Your confidence and growth must be developed by you, not by friends, family, or even professional counselors. When it is all said and done, you are the one who creates and maintains your self-image.

If we do it ourselves, then we own it. If we try to give someone else the responsibility, it will ultimately fail because we have not bought in. We must gain confidence in ourselves and solidify our own self-image. The affections and involvement of others will be helpful but will not ultimately accomplish the goal. We can do it ourselves, make sure it is done consistently, and develop the ability to maintain what we accomplish.

As we implement self-love we gain confidence in ourselves. Sometimes confidence is half the battle. When we do it, we experience the positive result, and that encourages us to maintain the necessary acts to accomplish our goal. We will never feel confident unless we do it ourselves.

Knowing we can make changes and improve our situation allows us to take risks and get out of our comfort zone. We will know we can get life back on track ourselves if we run into a difficult season in life. Learning to love yourself, encourage yourself, and build up yourself will help you in establishing a positive self-image.

Self-care is an act of self-love. These two terms are not necessarily the same, although some writers will use them interchangeably.

Self-care

The term self-care covers all the actions you take to care for yourself. Examples might include pampering, resting, journaling, meditation or prayer, exercise, or relaxation. You are looking after the physical, emotional, and mental aspect of yourself. You have certain inherent needs and you take care of them, rather than ignore them.

Self-love

Self-love is a different and more complicated subject. While acts of self-care typically are short-term and immediate in nature, self-love is the long-term and more permanent, ongoing version of taking care of yourself.

Self-love has more to do with what you believe and how you feel about yourself rather than the actual acts of doing something to provide an immediate benefit. The ultimate goal is unconditional love for yourself. It's like the unconditional love you have for your marriage partner. It is not going to change regardless of the circumstances.

Implementing self-love practices allows you to be good to yourself while in the process of building and solidifying your self-image.

POSITIVE SELF-TALK

1. Forgive yourself

It is very easy to blame yourself for mistakes, poor judgment, or for arriving at a place in your life where you are not happy. Forgive yourself! Would you forgive another person who did something that hurt you or created problems for you? Forgiving yourself is no different that forgiving a friend.

When you are angry or feel resentment towards others, it often is more damaging to you than it is to the other party. Forgiveness is really more for the benefit of the one forgiving than the one being forgiven. The strain of holding onto anger or being resentful is far more damaging to the one with such feelings. Frequently the other person doesn't even know of the hurt or has long forgotten it.

2. Be compassionate toward yourself

Be compassionate with yourself as you would be compassionate with others. You deserve your own best efforts. Help yourself grow, change, and improve. Why would you want to neglect your own well-being?

If you are being hard on yourself, make a list of all your good qualities identifying the kindnesses you have bestowed on others.

3. Admit problems and move on

Don't let problems weigh you down. Recognize the problem, fix it, monitor how you are doing, and then let go of it. Continuing to hold on to problems, embarrassments, or difficulties is not helpful.

Negative self-talk is not productive. You can find yourself wallowing in a pool of negative thoughts and actions that are like dried mud on a pig – it's hard to shake off. Focusing on bad decisions for long periods is a waste of time and energy. There is nothing to be gained.

Spend time on positive events and think about how they should shape your identity. What can you do today that would be positive and help erase the thoughts dragging you down?

4. You have the power

Don't allow others to make your decisions. Others may have good intentions but they are not you. You call the shots for you so make sure what you are doing is consistent with your agenda and not someone else's. You have the power to build and improve your self-image and identity.

Don't let someone else usurp that power. You are in charge. It is your life and you have the power and ability to fix or improve it.

5. Have a plan and work it

Think and plan what you are doing. God gave us a brain. We should use it. Consider and evaluate alternatives. Spend time thinking about what you want to achieve. Consider your strengths and how you can use them to change or improve your situation.

If it is time to think about new things, don't be held back by past events. Focus on where you are strong, valuable, and have the ability to contribute. Consider subjects that build you up, not tear you down.

6. Be grateful

Be grateful, particularly toward yourself. A grateful life is a happy life. Think about and consider what you have to be thankful for. Put your heart and mind into a place of thankfulness. See item #8 in Chapter 8 for additional comments about being grateful.

7. Be loving and caring

Just as you can live with an attitude of gratitude, you can live with an attitude of love, compassion, and caring for yourself and others. If you don't love yourself it will be difficult to love others. Helping others will do amazing things for your self-image.

Love is not necessarily a skill or ability, but rather it is a decision. You <u>choose</u> to offer someone friendship or love. You can decide that it is given without any strings and without expectation of some future gain. You may not find it easy, but the recipient will be encouraged and grateful for your care.

You receive the knowledge and positive feelings of helping or caring for another person. It is a feeling that is never forgotten and may be savored for a lifetime.

8. Use Kind Words

Celebrate success with words that build yourself up, no matter how small the result. Recognize the good things you have done and the good things that are going on around you. Celebrate those things with positive affirmations.

Remind yourself regularly that you are worthy of honor, respect, and love. This will go a long way in combatting the false impression you may have about yourself.

Following are three affirmations that you might use:

1. I am in charge of my own destiny. Others can help, but I am in charge.
2. No outside influence can damage my identity. I determine my own self-image.
3. My value or self-worth is not determined by my successes, failures, or the opinions of others.

Never forget to treat yourself right. If you ignore the positive occurrences in life it's easy to fall into the bad habit of dwelling on the negative. Consider the good and give yourself a pat on the back. If the good was particularly effective, make the reward valuable enough that you will want to do it again.

9. Believe in yourself

If you don't believe in yourself, nobody else is likely to take a chance. People who have little confidence in themselves usually display that to others. Body language and speech give your secret away pretty quickly. Sometime the symptoms can be hidden for a while but they are eventually obvious to others – you don't really believe you can do it!

If your confidence quotient is low, do things that you know you can succeed at. Take classes or training to improve skills that will give you confidence in your abilities.

Having a network of people who can and will help you overcome issues and problems is a great benefit. Some even consider a life coach or life counselor to help with certain self-image or identity issues that are difficult.

"Relentless, repetitive self-talk
is what changes our self-image."
Denis Waitley[43]

TIPS YOU COULD USE

a. Underline, circle, or highlight the tips, ideas, or concepts above that you think would make the most impact if you implemented them in your life. You will revisit these choices at the end of the book in the planning section.

b. There may be other ideas that you think could improve your self-image. Write them below:

_____

_____

_____

_____

SELF-LOVE AND SELF-CARE ACTIVITIES

> *"There is overwhelming evidence that*
> *the higher the level of self-esteem,*
> *the more likely one will be to treat*
> *others with respect, kindness, and generosity."*
> Nathaniel Branden[44]

Following is a general list of ideas and actions you can take that can improve your self-esteem, self-image, and ultimately your identity. It is long enough that you should be able to find something that would work in your life.

Don't fall into the trap of thinking every idea in this list will work for you. You may already be doing some of them.

Some may not fit your personality. But there are many gems in this list that will work for you. Good hunting.

1. Accept yourself and your situation

Don't try to change things that can't be changed. You may have to work next to someone whom you do not like or who irritates you. You may have to put up with that person for a season in your life. Everything you do and all your circumstances will not be the best all the time. Be patient: this too will pass. Learn to live with the difficult seasons of life and recognize that by accepting these seasons you are growing in your self-identity.

Change the things that can be changed and ignore those over which you have no control.

2. Trust yourself

Trust is a very important element of self-love. If you don't trust yourself, who do you trust? Worry and anxiety can tamper with your heart and your mind. The advice of others is often valuable and should be sought out when help is needed. Just remember that you make the decisions for your life.

Trusting yourself is a great way to practice self-love. Trust can be a leap of faith. Do things that are good for you; that allow you to grow and mature. Listen to your inner self talk when it says to step out in faith.

No one else knows your needs and ways as well as you do. Get input from others but do not allow them to make your decisions. If you are having serious mental or emotional problems you may need professional help or advice.

*"Trust yourself. You know more
than you think you do."*
Benjamin Spock[45]

3. It's a journey: be kind to yourself and have fun!

Don't forget this is *your* life. Keep your focus on your needs if you want to build up your self-image. Do what makes sense for you. Don't copy other people. Pick and choose what will work for you and your lifestyle.

Remember self-love is a journey, not the end result. The path will be up and down. There will be obstacles that must be overcome. Some days will be difficult or challenging. Set your sights on the destination and continue to practice self-care and self-love. Accept the fact that the road may have some potholes.

Don't beat yourself up when you run into a problem. Keep focused on the journey and on making progress toward a positive self-image.

Make life enjoyable. Learn to like yourself and to treat yourself well. Try new things. Focus on your enjoyment. You are worth it. Take vacations. Go to new places where the focus is on having fun. Put aside work and family responsibilities to refresh and relax.

4. Take care of yourself

Taking care of yourself plays a big role in self-love. Let go of all the regrettable, humiliating, or foolish things you may have done at some point in your life. Keep your eyes on the future and give yourself some grace. You have much to offer others.

Your well-being includes the full range of physical, mental, and emotional health. Allow time for proper exercise, eating the right foods, and getting enough rest. Don't allow alcohol and drugs to destroy your life. Mood-altering substances can ruin all the good things you are doing to improve your self-image.

5. You can't control everything

Accept the fact that some things are outside your ability to change. Focus on how to respond to life, rather than control or change it.

6. Don't be influenced

Stop wasting your time on the Internet and social media. Don't allow talking heads to influence you into thinking negatively about anything. Influencers have one objective: to influence you to do something <u>they</u> want you to do for <u>their</u> benefit. It's not about you. It's about them.

7. Remember who you are

You are whoever you want to be. Don't let others create a negative picture of yourself. You can control and weather the adverse times in life. Everyone must deal with challenges. Show others your resilience and don't allow the setbacks in your life define you. Know who you really are and rely on your strengths.

8. Don't stifle your creativity

Creative people can sometimes have trouble expressing themselves if they are struggling with questions about their abilities and self-image. Creativity can be stifled by low self-esteem. Park your inner criticism at the curb and allow yourself to be creative. Whatever your interest— painting, writing, sculpting, constructing, music—begin spending quality time with your creative side.

9. Immerse yourself in what you enjoy

If you like to read, read what you like, not necessarily what you think is good for you. Listen to music. I personally love to take thirty minutes to listen and watch my favorite singers on YouTube. That may not excite you, but I come away at peace. Do what works for you.

Surrounding yourself with things you like can apply to all aspects of life. Don't spend time with people that make you uncomfortable. Don't have a job that you hate. Don't go to concerts that you find boring. Don't go clubbing because someone else loves it.

Do what brings you joy.

Pursue your passions. Avoid participating in activities you don't enjoy. You deserve the joy of participating in activities that bring you happiness and excitement. Even if you are not good at an activity, just do it to treat yourself. Avoid things you strongly dislike. If you can't ride a horse and it scares you to death, don't do it. If you like to knit, get your yarn out and do it.

Celebrate special occasions and accomplishments, even if they are small. Be happy with what you have done and what you have achieved. Be pleased with yourself whenever it is warranted. Be kind to yourself.

YOUR ATTITUDE IS A KEY

You can't love yourself if you don't like who you are. Hardships, suffering, abuse, and toxic relationships can do great damage to your self-esteem. Self-esteem that has been damaged by serious negative consequences can be regained but it may not be easy and it may not happen quickly. You must be patient and persevere. You are worth it, even if you don't feel that way at the present moment.

Don't allow the hardships in life to dictate your well-being. When you make a mistake, fix it and move on. Don't brood over it for weeks or months on end. Everyone makes mistakes. Many of us grow and mature the most after making a mistake. Forgive yourself because you are worth a do-over!

Look forward to life with anticipation, but on your terms. It's okay not to do everything anyone asks. Say "No" when the request is not conducive to your well-being or when you have no real free time. Your schedule can become a source of great consternation if you don't manage it well.

Any number of occurrences can get in the way of living life. Your attitude toward life and its challenges is a key to overcoming difficulties and celebrating victories. Following are some suggestions for living life with a good attitude.

1. Have empathy and compassion for others

Give attention to those situations where a good word, a helping hand, or a soft shoulder will bring comfort or joy. Giving help to others is guaranteed to lift your spirits and self-esteem. When you open your heart to others they are likely to do the same for you, but don't be compassionate just to receive some reciprocal kindness.

Compassion for others, meeting the needs of others, helping them achieve something important, or just helping them out of a difficulty *will bring you great joy and satisfaction*. It will nourish your self-image. It will bolster your self-worth which will often cause you to do greater things to improve your perception of yourself.

2. Ignore the feeling to be perfect

No one should seek perfection. If someone is selling perfection, that's the first clue to ignore whatever they are saying. No one is perfect or even near perfect (although some people may think they are)! We all have flaws and we need to live with them. Yes, trying to improve oneself is certainly appropriate, but thinking you can get near perfection is idiocy. We all have flaws we must live with.

3. Ignore the unrealistic standards of others

You are what you are. You are unique and you have a unique set of skills and abilities. Avoid trying to meet goals set by others. You cannot reach unattainable goals that someone else sets for you. You are the master of your heart, mind, and soul. Don't let others take that away.

4. Live for today

Stop the continuing search for something better. Better is not always best. Certainly having life goals is important but a consistent quest for something better is not necessary a good mindset. Your self-worth is not determined by achieving a better you. Your worth is a function of what you do for others.

5. Think positive thoughts

If you are having negative thoughts, do something good for yourself. Don't ignore how you are feeling and thinking. Stay in touch with your feelings and stop the negative thinking. Here are several ways to control negative thoughts:

- Don't be surprised by them. We all have negative thoughts from time to time. Don't dwell on them or spend lots of time trying to overcome them.
- Challenge your negative thinking with positive and realistic truth.
- Be prepared to cope with the negative comments and attitudes of others.
- Don't judge yourself. Yes, everyone does things they regret, but that doesn't mean you must continually be focused on negative experiences. Find ways to cope and change your mind-set.
- When negative feelings and thoughts arise, think about the positive things you have done.

6. Don't be critical of yourself

You will not always be right. Your work may not always be the best. You will make mistakes. So what? We are all learning and you will make mistakes if you try new things or try to improve. Don't stop because something you want to do doesn't seem to be working out right.

Don't be overly critical of yourself. Remember, most skills are learned, they are not God given talents. Even those people with natural abilities must work at their gifts in order to make them special.

7. Test and redefine your comfort zone

Don't be trapped by the same routines because you are uncomfortable doing something new. Being bored by your life activities can lead to a lower self-image. It's fun and exciting to be successful at new things. It's even fun making mistakes because it's new and different. Don't bore yourself into a poor self-image.

8. Avoid seeking approval

It does not matter what you are doing, somebody is not going to like it and somebody will think you should do it differently. Don't do anything for the mere purpose of pleasing someone else. Once you let go of a need to please others, it will become easier to avoid doing things just because others think you should.

9. Be realistic

No one feels upbeat all the time. No one is always happy. Expect to have bad days. But don't let the bad days, bad events, or bad situations control your life. The bad can be fixed: make it right and move on. Don't be overly hard on yourself. Be realistic in your expectations for yourself and others.

TIPS YOU COULD USE

a. Underline, circle, or highlight the activities or attitudes in the two sections above that you think would make the most impact in your life. You will revisit these choices at the end of the book in the planning section.

b. There may be other ideas that you think could improve your self-image. Write them below:

_____

_____

_____

_____

RELATIONSHIPS

The choice of friends and relationships can be influenced by a number of factors:

- Your family and how your parents raised you.
- Where you grew up (city/rural, ethnic neighborhood, etc.)
- Who taught you right from wrong.
- How you were treated, disciplined, and loved as a child.
- The intimacy in your family.
- What your parents, siblings, teachers, and mentors modeled as good behavior – not what they said but what they did.

What standards do you have for relationships? Do you have any spoken or unspoken characteristics that must be present before you will pursue a serious relationship?

How do relationships affect your self-image and self-esteem? In thinking about relationships it will be beneficial to consider the following:

- ACCEPTANCE: Are you accepted or are you ignored or even rejected?
- TRUST: Is the relationship one of trust and dependability or is it untrustworthy, unreliable, and undependable?
- COMFORT: Are you comfortable and open with the other person or group, or are you constantly on guard and anxious about what might be said or done next?
- CONTROL: Does the relationship foster individualism or is it controlling how you are expected to act? Are you to conform to some set of rules or expectations? Are you a slave to someone, something, some idea, or some cause?
- OPEN and FREE: Does the relationship foster togetherness or does it encourage separate activities intended to isolate or create an environment of separation?
- INDEPENDENCE: Does the relationship encourage self-reliance and celebrate independent thought and accomplishments or does it create and encourage dependence on someone or something?

Independence means you don't need permission to do anything: you determine your own values and priorities. You stand on your own and answer for yourself.

"One of the greatest regrets in life is being
what others would want you to be,
rather than being yourself."
Shannon L. Alder

1. Accept compassion from others

What happens when others offer you help? If you believe you're the strong one or that you don't need help, an offer of help you might be difficult to accept.

As we have said elsewhere in this book, your problems are probably not a secret to your friends and family. Co-workers and bosses also might be aware of your struggles. Don't react negatively to offers of help. They love and care for you or they would not make such an offer.

Whatever the nature of the gesture, it will probably mean you need to lower your guard a bit and be gracious. Your response might be a simple hug or it might be appropriate to share something personal. Allow others to love you. It will likely be as beneficial for them as it is for you.

2. Surround yourself with good people

Don't keep friends who don't treat you well. Seek out people who respect and honor you; people you can trust. Negative voices do nothing for your self-esteem. Positive people will spur you on to greater things and look after your interests.

Don't be afraid to seek help when you need it. Seeking help is not a sign of weakness but rather recognizing when going it alone is not the best course of action.

3. Choose good friends and associates

It may be necessary to cull or add to your social circle. Are you spending time with the right people? Do you need to drop or add people to your group of associates or friends? If there are those in your group who are negative, insulting, or just bring you down, drop them from your circle of friends. That may sound harsh, but you must do it. Remember, you owe destructive people no allegiance.

Stop all toxic relationships immediately. There is no reason to allow toxic people in your life. You want people around you who care and support you. Don't spend any more time with people who don't really care about you. Find people whom you like and like you.

4. Treat others well.

You will feel good about yourself if your treat others with honor and respect. Treat others the way you would want to be treated.

SPECIAL ACTIVITIES

1. Have a plan

Planning is too important of a subject to ignore. Without a plan you might just coast along and not ever get to where you want to be. It is simply a matter of putting some structure to something you want to accomplish. A plan will give you the best chance of making real progress and achieving your goals.

Regardless of whether you complete the planning process at the end of this book, you need to define and record an outline of the actions you want to take. You could put this on a legal pad, a leather-bound planner, or on your phone. The important thing is to get it in writing! Periodically evaluate your progress and update your outline.

2. Schedule a quiet time

A quiet time can be one of the most effective self-love activities that your adopt. Spend time thinking about things that are greater than yourself. What are your life priorities and are you being steadfast? Are you making progress toward your life goals? Have you transgressed against any of your core values?

A quiet time can also be used to settle your heart and mind and concentrate on thinking about something you love. You might also turn on soothing music. This is not a time to listen to the latest rock music.

Clear your mind and think good thoughts. Dream dreams if you like. Imagine the impossible and then ask if it is really impossible. Encourage yourself with positive self-talk.

3. Practice journaling

Commit to journaling for the next three to six months. Practice writing down important and new ideas as well as recording your feelings. Write about your experiences and how you think they impact your identity.

Create a daily list of significant accomplishments. Comment in your journal why the accomplishment was successful. What did you do that made the event happen? Your journal can act as a vision board where you record goals, dreams, plans, and actions you want to take.

4. Try new pursuits

Try new things from time to time. Don't be stuck in the same rut. Get a friend to join you if you need encouragement. Challenge yourself. What are you capable of? Get serious about a hobby or a long-abandoned activity. Take a leap of faith if necessary. What is the real consequence if you fail or don't achieve your objective? Falling short is probably not as bad as you may think.

5. Periodically run a self-check

How are you doing? How do you feel about yourself? Are you working your plan to love and care for yourself? Are you having mood swings? Why? Is there something in your life you need to fix or get under control? Grab a hot or cold drink, get comfortable and review your progress in building up your self-image.

6. Keep moving

Don't sit in one spot for more than an hour. Move around to get your body relaxed and awake. Take up a sport. Go to a gym if that is your preference, or just walk around the block. Do something that will put some tone in your muscles. Becoming an exercise fanatic is not necessary – just keep moving.

7. De-clutter your life

Minimalism is something you might consider if your life is cluttered, too busy, or you can't seem to find any time for yourself. Material possessions can sometime get in the way of a healthy lifestyle. If you have too much stuff, get rid of some of it. It can take up so much of your time you are never able to get anything worthwhile accomplished.

Be happy and content with what you have. Perhaps resolve not to buy anything for six months. If you are particularly drawn to certain types of possessions, focus your time on shutting down those acquisitions so that life can return to normalcy.

8. Don't stop learning

Exercise your cognitive abilities. Try new things. Improve your skills. Don't sit on the sidelines watching. The real enjoyment is playing the game. Find ways to engage your mind in learning new things.

9. Manage stress

Everyone experiences stress. When you are in a stressful situation, do things that will relieve the worry and anxiety. Here are ten quick and easy stress relievers:

- Meditate or pray for 5-10 minutes.
- Treat yourself to some chocolate.
- Get 8-10 hours of sleep.
- Go for a 10 minute walk, or take a hike.
- Have a picnic with your favorite foods and drink.
- Do deep breathing exercises.
- Watch a funny video or listen to music.
- Write yourself a positive message.

Spending short periods utilizing a stress-management technique can be very beneficial. Stress prevention is important because it can impact health conditions like heart disease, obesity, and high blood pressure.

10. Visit your happy place

Not everyone has a special place where they feel comfortable and content, but if you have one, use it

IDENTITY LIFE PRINCIPLE: Be confident in who you are.

whenever it is needed. Special places of peace and good memories can lift your soul above the noise of daily difficulties. Make this place a regular part of your healthy and uplifting routines. If you don't have one, be on the lookout for it.

11. Laugh

Do things that make you laugh. Laughing is very healthy.

TIPS YOU COULD USE

a. Underline, circle, or highlight the tips, ideas, or concepts above that you think would make the most impact if you implemented them in your life. You will revisit these choices at the end of the book in the planning section.

b. There may be other ideas that you think could improve your self-image. Write them below:

_____

_____

_____

_____

_____

_____

*"Whatever you are doing, love yourself
for doing it. Whatever you are feeling,
love yourself for feeling it."*

Thaddeus Golas[47]

Wisdom to Action Challenge

Since this chapter consists of tips, select one tip to focus on each day of the week. Take the time to consider the tip in the morning, and be aware of opportunities to put it into practice throughout the day. Record your experiences and insights in a journal.

Chapter 12
Benefits of a
Positive Self-Image

*"Too many people overvalue what they
are not and undervalue what they are."*
Malcolm S. Forbes[48]

It is far easier to discuss or preach self-love than it is to practice it. It's often far easier to find fault than find strength and courage. When it is time to perform and actually do something, we can lose heart, hold back, or just not proceed with what we know we need to do.

Thus, it is important to be alert to negative self-talk and negative influences that will keep us from undertaking improvements in our lives. A positive self-image is a very desirable goal and state of mind. We inherently know that negative influences are detrimental, we just have trouble moving ahead toward a more positive mindset.

That's why in the next section of this book we begin a planning process that will help you know specifically what you want to do and assist you in getting started.

GENERAL

Before we begin the planning process, let's review the benefits of a positive self-image. Four *basic* benefits are:

- Improved health.
- Positive personal relationships.
- Satisfaction, peace, and contentment.
- Increased self-esteem.

Remember, other people will often treat us just like we treat ourselves. If it appears we don't like ourselves, other people will pick up on that attitude. When others see us being good to ourselves, they will tend to treat us the same way.

Many believe that positive identity and self-image is an important key to *lasting* success and satisfaction. Remember, if you don't like yourself, why would you expect anyone else to give you much help in improving your self-image? Others don't want to get in the middle of your problems.

There are many benefits to a positive self-image, some of which are very significant. But don't believe that a positive self-image will solve all of life's problems and challenges. There are many beneficial aspects of a positive self-image but feeling good and having confidence in your abilities will not necessarily solve all your problems.

We will not go into great detail in the following benefits but will provide a brief outline of what you can expect if you try to improve your self-image.

TWELVE MAJOR BENEFITS

1. Positive attitude
You will be more satisfied and content, upbeat, optimistic, enthusiastic, happy, and pleasant. You won't feel driven to engage in self-destructive habits or behavior. This does not

mean you no longer have problems and issues, but they no longer will hold you hostage to destructive behavior.

2. Core values
You have the ability to define and maintain your core values. They will no longer feel elusive and impossible. You will have more confidence in living up to the standards you have set for yourself.

3. Decision-making
A positive self-image will help you make more intelligent decisions. These decisions will be beneficial to living a more satisfied and successful life.

4. Attitude
Your attitude will move toward the positive and you will tend to feel grateful for your blessings rather than depressed about your shortcomings or disappointments. You will be able to take responsibility for your attitude, thoughts, and behavior. Integrity will become important along with other positive character traits.

5. Emotional stability
A positive self-image gives you better emotional stability. You will be able to handle disappointments better. Flaws in your life will not seem overwhelming and you will take control of your life.

6. Control
Many life problems tend to fade away with a positive self-image. You will have more self-control over more facets of your life and lifestyle. You will be less volatile and will bounce back from problems more quickly.

7. Accomplishments

You will have more frequent successes. You will come to understand how to maximize your time and talents. You may experience a new willingness to try new things. You will learn and grow from both failures and successes.

8. Relationships

You will tend to get more cooperation from others and your personal relationships will improve. You should have an increased empathy for others and be more tolerant and forgiving. You will not be threatened by other people's achievements.

9. Job performance

Good or better job performance should be evident. Confidence and a positive self-image are very beneficial in working hard and working smart.

10. Health

Good health and well-being should result from a more positive attitude. You will be able to manage and better handle stress. Deepak Chopra[49] has said, "The power of positive self-image plays a vital role in experiencing perfect health." You will not allow poor health habits to control your life.

11. Body-image

You can overcome negative body-image issues when you understand the truth, the reality of your appearance, the true importance of your appearance, and the associated body-image issues. You'll find it much easier to focus on what is important and not on lies or misunderstandings about body-image.

12. Addictions

You can avoid or overcome addictions. Addictions are often caused or encouraged by a poor or negative self-image. Drugs and alcohol are often used to hide a bad self-image. Once the negative perceptions are corrected, the use of alcohol and drugs are not needed.

"There are so many more important things to worry about than how you're perceived by strangers."
Dennis Lehane[50]

Wisdom to Action Challenge

Choose one of the twelve major benefits discussed above that you want to experience in your life. Identify five things you could do to help that benefit occur in your life and do one each day this week.

Chapter 13

Planning Part 1
Life Analysis

———

IDENTITY LIFE PRINCIPLE
Be confident in who you are.

INTRODUCTION

The objective of this Life Analysis chapter is to survey your life situation for information that will be used in later chapters to identify your core values, life priorities, commitments, and goals. In Chapter 16 we will formulate action steps to make having a positive self-image be a reality in your life.

If you have already read one of the other books in this series and completed the Life Analysis in that book, the questions and exercises are the same, but your answers are about a different subject. However, some of your responses will be the same or similar and you might want to have that book handy as you complete this Life Analysis.

Most of us have never done any kind of extensive self-examination and certainly not thought about writing down the results. I can tell you personally there is much to be gained from writing them down rather than just thinking, talking, or meditating about them. It will give you a clear picture of your life and help you evaluate what you really want to accomplish.

The focus of this book is to address <u>one</u> particular topic in your life. It is not a complete life plan. A complete and detailed Life Plan is the subject of our *Life Planning Handbook*. See the "Next Steps" page at the end of this book for more information.

Our life planning process has five primary parts which we will cover in the following chapters.

Chapter 13, Part 1
>Life Analysis: What is your life situation today?

Chapter 14, Part 2
>Life Values: What is important to you?

Chapter 15, Part 3
>Life Principle Goals: What are your objectives?

Chapter 16, Part 4
>Action Steps: How do you get from where you are today to your goals?

Chapter 17, Part 5
>Ongoing Progress Review: How are you doing?

Life planning is not a difficult process. It will certainly be easier for those who have thought about these questions before. You might even have an existing plan of some kind. If so, this will be a good check on where you are and how you are doing. If you have a plan, it would be worthwhile pulling it out as you progress through the remaining parts of this book.

If you don't know where you're going,
any path will get you there!

I don't know the source of this quote but I have had it emblazoned in my brain since my college days. I think it came from one of my college business classes or textbooks. I have heard it repeated a number of times over the years, primarily because it is so true.

If you don't know your destination, then any choice of roads at all the forks in life will be an acceptable choice. It won't really matter which road you take because you don't have a destination in mind anyway. And when you get there you won't know you have arrived.

We need a purpose, a destination, and priorities so we are not wandering aimlessly through life. Even if you are not a "planning person," be assured we will walk you through every step. Knowing your path is important because:

1) Every path leads somewhere.

2) The life-road on which you are traveling, the direction in which you are heading, and your expected destination <u>will</u> determine your life.

3) You cannot allow apathy, other people, or chance to determine either your path or your destination.

Without purpose and direction it is difficult to make good choices. Just thinking about the questions we will ask in the following process will be helpful. Our planning process should produce these positive results:

- it will create focus, attention, and desire,
- it will cause action – doing something,
- it will begin to establish the importance of what you believe,
- it will help you make better decisions,
- it will help reduce distractions and hindrances, and
- it will motivate you.

> *"Life is not easy for any of us.*
> *But what of that? We must have*
> *perseverance and above all confidence*
> *in ourselves. We must believe that we*
> *are gifted for something and this thing*
> *must be attained."*
> Marie Curie[51]

LIFE ANALYSIS – KNOW YOURSELF

The first step in any form of life planning is to know and understand where you are today. What is your current situation? What is impacting your decisions and ultimately your life today? The first objective will be to identify your present situation and circumstances. Before we begin, take note of the following suggestions:

1. During this process you may find that you draw a blank on a particular question. If that happens, move on to the next question and return to the unanswered ones at a later time.

2. These questions relate specifically to the Identity Life Principle which is focused on your self-image and being confident in who you are. If that limited scope makes it difficult to answer any particular question, then answer from a broader life perspective if you think it would be helpful. If the question doesn't apply in any significant way, leave it blank.

3. You might find it convenient to write your initial responses in a separate notebook or computer and transfer that information to this book after you have thought about it and modified it to accurately reflect your thoughts and circumstances. Regardless of how you develop your answers, keep your notes, as they may be useful at a later date.

4. Remember, you are developing a plan focused on the Identity Life Principle, not on your life in general. Therefore, your responses should be focused on that subject.

KNOW YOURSELF – Interests
INSTRUCTION: What are the things and activities you love to do? What gives you joy as related to the Identity Life Principle?

1.

_____

2.

_____

3.

_____

4.

_____

5.

_____

KNOW YOURSELF – Skills

INSTRUCTION: What are your greatest physical or mental skills and abilities related to the Identity Life Principle?

1.

_____

2.

_____

3.

_____

4.

_____

5.

_____

KNOW YOURSELF – Strengths

INSTRUCTION: What are your strengths, special skills, and passions in regard to the Identity Life Principle?

1.

_____

2.

_____

3.

_____

4.

_____

5.

_____

KNOW YOURSELF – Weaknesses

INSTRUCTION: What are your weaknesses in regard to the Identity Life Principle?

1.

_____

2.

_____

3.

_____

4.

_____

5.

_____

KNOW YOURSELF – Roadblocks

Who or what things do you fear the most? What are the roadblocks, distractions, and hindrances that might prevent you from improving your life in any way? Circle any that might apply and add your own in the empty boxes.

Disabilities	Failure	Bankruptcy	Divorce	Loss of job
Public speaking	Confrontation	War	Loss of friends	Peer pressure
Poor health	My boss	Guilt	No legacy	God
Time	Apathy	Relationships	Death	Family
Inability to stand firm	Immoral behavior	Unethical behavior	Lack of skills and abilities	Emotions and feelings
Fears and insecurities	Lack purpose in life	Lack of Core values	Lack of patience	Improper motives
Bad habits				

INSTRUCTION: Based on what you circled above, record any serious roadblocks or hindrances that could prevent you from achieving the Identity Life Principle. Indicate the reason they are roadblocks.

1.

_____

2.

_____

3.

_____

4.

_____

KNOW YOURSELF – Character

How would you evaluate your personal character? Do you have any serious character flaws (your religious friends might refer to these as sins)? If you have any serious character flaws in your life, you may need to deal with them in order to make real progress toward the Identity Life Principle objective.

INSTRUCTION: Circle the positive traits which you lack and the existence of character flaws that might hinder your ability to achieve the Identity Life Principle.

LACK OF POSITIVE CHARACTER TRAITS:				
Honesty	Kindness	Caring	Forgiving	Goodness
Hopeful	Humility	Dependable	Loving	Diligence
Respectful	Godly	Patient	Generous	Satisfied
Peace	Merciful	Trustworthy	Self-controlled	Thankful
Devout	Disciplined	Obedient	Gentle	Prudent
Sincerity	Fair/Just	Grateful		
EXISTING CHARACTER FLAWS:				
Bad language	Boastfulness	Gossip	Slanderous	Lying
Cheating	Stubbornness	Anger	Hostility	Fear
Foolishness	Mischievousness	Rebellion	Hypocrisy	Envy
Unruliness	Ingratitude	Pride	Immorality	Addictions
Jealousy	Bitterness	Hatred	Unforgiving	Shame
Respect	Deceitfulness	Deceit	Vanity	Revenge

The above list is not exhaustive. If there are other issues you should add, write them in the empty boxes above.

INSTRUCTION: Review the issues you have identified and list anything below that could <u>seriously</u> hinder achieving the Identity Life Principle. List the issue and how it would negatively impact your ability to achieve your objectives.

1.

_____

_____

2.

_____

_____

3.

_____

_____

KNOW YOURSELF – Conclusion

This concludes your information gathering. You should now have at your fingertips a good overview of who you are and what might impact your ability to achieve the Identity LIfe Principle, both good and bad.

The next step in the process of knowing yourself is to use this information to determine your core values, life priorities, and life commitments.

Chapter 14

Planning Part 2
Life Values

IDENTITY LIFE PRINCIPLE

Be confident in who you are.

CORE VALUES

What are the standards by which you live? What values do you cherish? What do you believe in? What values or standards will you absolutely not compromise or violate? The latter are your *core values*.

Self-assessment and full understanding of yourself and your environment must begin with identifying and knowing your core values. Core values are the principles, standards, or beliefs that are so important to you that you would not violate them. They will dictate your most important decisions and help you choose your direction.

You don't need to have your whole life figured out, but you do need to know what matters most to you. You need to know your ethical and moral standards. What issues or actions do you believe in so strongly that you would be deeply ashamed if you violated them? These are values and principles you believe in and live by, and to the best of your ability you will not forsake them. They represent who you really are. They are your core values.

If you are a religious person you might have a core value that indicates you would stand firm on your religious principles, and you might name them. If you love and seek intellectual improvement you might have a core value related to seeking and gaining knowledge and wisdom. If you are a dedicated parent you probably have core values related to your children or parenting.

Core values may change or become more or less important as you age and the path of your life journey changes.

You may be aware of several of your core values but you probably have never written them down. This exercise will be an important step in understanding yourself and what is important to you.

If this is a new subject for you, you might start by looking at all the topics on the "Life Planning Series" page (prior to Chapter 1) and determine if any of those subjects represent core values for you.

There are other subjects that might be appropriate for you to consider, for example: wisdom, influence, health, leadership, security, fitness, family, volunteer service, ethics, joy, relationships, moderation, balance, justice/injustice, addictions, laws, safety, etc.

Your core values should cover the things that are important to you. For example, you might have a core value of: "I will always try to do what is right and I will teach my children to do what is right, even if it is uncomfortable." Or, you might have a core value related to money: "I will never spend more than I earn. I will pay off credit cards monthly."

FINAL CORE VALUES

Develop these values based on a total life perspective, not just the Identity Life Principle, and make them work for you. If you have never thought about this before, we recommend you begin with 5 to 8, but no more than twelve. This is a critical step in this planning exercise, so spend sufficient time thinking and evaluating your final choices. Remember, core values are those values or standards that you will absolutely not compromise or violate.

INSTRUCTION: Develop your list of core values and record them here. We suggest you try to list twelve and then cut the list back to the best 5 to 8.

1. _____

2. _____

3. _____

4. _____

5. _____

6. _____

7. _____

8. _____

9. _____

10. _____

11. _____

12. _____

Do any of the core values you listed above relate to your self-image? If not, do you need one? You may not, but don't leave it off because you overlooked the obvious. You may want to include one in order to give your objectives for the Identity Life Principle more focus and importance at this time.

LIFE VALUES: Priorities (initial list)

Our perspective in this exercise is your total life, not just the Identity Life Principle.

What are the things that are very important to you today? What are your life priorities? Where do you currently spend your money and your time? What do you spend your life doing and thinking about? For this initial list of priorities, ignore anything new that you may be considering relative to living a better life. Record just your priorities today (the good and the bad).

If you do something daily or regularly, then it is probably a priority. If you average more than an hour a day doing something, it's also probably a priority. What do you regularly spend money on? Assuming you have a normal 8:00 – 5:00 job, what do you do in the evenings and on weekends?

You might have Life Priorities related to your spiritual life, the educational system where you live, the ethical standards of your friends, your health and diet, hobbies, raising your children, your marriage, your times of pleasure and relaxation, politics, volunteer service, your work ethic, saving money, immorality, your job or career, where you will live, your personal growth, etc.

INSTRUCTION: What are your actual top 6 to 12 life priorities today? Record them here based on a total life perspective.

1.

2.

3.

4.

5.

6.

7.

8.

9.

10.

_____

11.

_____

12.

_____

ISSUES – URGENCY:
If you learned that you had only two years of life left, what impact would that have on your Life Priorities? How might they change?

_____

_____

_____

_____

_____

_____

ISSUES – SACRIFICES AND RISKS:
What new risks or sacrifices would you have to make in order to accomplish the Identity Life Principle? Would that change your current Life Priorities?

_____

_____

_____

_____

_____

ISSUES – KNOWING YOURSELF:

Look back over the "Life Analysis – Know Yourself" and determine if there is anything that should change or be added to your Life Priorities.

_____

_____

_____

_____

_____

ISSUES – LIVING A BETTER LIFE:

Given a desire to adopt the Identity Life Principle for your life, what new priorities would you need to adopt? Ask yourself what you must absolutely do in order to successfully live a better life. What new priorities does that create and how would any existing priorities have to change?

_____

_____

_____

_____

_____

_____

_____

FINAL LIFE PRIORITIES

Prepare a complete list below of your new and revised total Life Priorities. Try to keep this list at 6 to 8, but no more than 12. You should intentionally include priorities that relate to the Identity Life Principle.

1.

_____

2.

_____

3.

_____

4.

_____

5.

_____

6.

_____

7.

_____

8.

_____

9.

_____

10.

_____

11.

_____

12.

_____

LIFE COMMITMENTS

Are these Commitments the same as Life Priorities? No! Your Life Priorities identify the _things that are very important_ to you, while Life Commitments are _things you must do_ to make Life Priorities a reality in your life. Life Commitments are sometimes useful if they focus on areas where you have particular difficulties.

It's very possible that there are new commitments you must make that are not directly related to the Identity Life Principle. For example, if your desire is to be honest you will also have to commit to being trustworthy, dependable, reliable, and loyal. If you want to be generous, then you can't love money. If you desire to guard your speech, then you cannot be out of control and let anger control your tongue. If you are going to live a life free of drugs, then you must commit to eliminating friends and associates who use drugs.

The point of these examples is to demonstrate that if you are serious about the Identity Life Principle, then automatically there will be other related commitments necessary to be successful.

You could have a commitment that says you are going to commit to having a positive self-image, but that doesn't really provide you with much help or focus. If one of your biggest problems is allowing others to bully you or take advantage of you, then a commitment to stand your ground or stand firm on your beliefs and recommendations becomes a far more meaningful commitment. If your difficulties often revolve around never asking others for help, you could commit to not making any important decision without getting input from at least two people. Try to make your commitments specific enough that they will be useful to you.

The important concept to recognize is that the Identity Life Principle will *automatically* require committing to one or more other behaviors and traits that are related to your self-image and may be troublesome if not an area of focus.

Since Life Priorities inherently identify your objectives, examine those priorities and determine the related commitments that you must make in order to achieve each Life Priority. The focus should be on what you must commit to in order to achieve the Identity Life Principle.

INSTRUCTION: List the traits, behaviors, activities, or habits that you must manage or control in order for you to achieve the Identity Life Principle (one or two words).

1. _____

2. _____

3. _____

4. _____

5. _____

6. _____

7. _____

8. _____

9. _____

10. _____

FINAL LIFE COMMITMENTS

INSTRUCTION: Based on the above, develop the Life Commitments you feel you should make in order to successfully achieve the Identity Life Principle. These should be significant commitments, therefore, select the 4 to 8 that would really help you improve your self-image.

"There's a difference between interest and commitment. When you are interested in doing something, you do it only when it's convenient. When you're committed to something, you accept no excuses, only results."
Kenneth Blanchard[52]

1. _____

_____

2. _____

_____

3. _____

_____

4.

_____

_____

5.

_____

_____

6.

_____

_____

7.

_____

_____

8.

_____

_____

Chapter 15

Planning Part 3
Life Goals

———

IDENTITY LIFE PRINCIPLE
Be confident in who you are.

"Life takes on meaning when you become motivated,
set goals and charge after them
in an unstoppable manner."
Les Brown[53]

Our Life Goal in this book is the Identity Life Principle: *I will be confident in my identity.* A complete plan would have other goals, but in this book we are focused only on the subject of self-image.

If it would be useful for you, you may want to note or record other Life Goals you already have or you want to make given the material you have read in this book.

Life Goals are your objectives for the future. They are influenced by your Core Values, Life Priorities, and your Life Commitments.

LIFE GOALS

INSTRUCTION: We have entered the Identity Life Principle goal, and you may list other personal goals, if you like.

1. *I will be confident in my identity.*

   OTHERS (for future use):

   2.

   _____

   3.

   _____

   4.

   _____

   5.

   _____

   6.

   _____

"Your ability to discipline yourself to set clear goals, and then to work toward them every day, will do more to guarantee your success than any other single factor."
Brian Tracy[54]

Chapter 16

Planning Part 4
Action Steps

IDENTITY LIFE PRINCIPLE
Be confident in who you are.

*If you want something to happen,
you will need to take action.*

INTRODUCTION

All the work in the previous chapters has given you a wealth of knowledge about where you are today and what you want to achieve in the future. You have even written it down. This is the point at which you actually take the step to determine what you are going to do about it.

As you think about what you need to do, include language that would allow you to measure your success or progress, if possible. Where appropriate, include the dates when you intend to begin and complete each step. The best action steps are those that can be measured, allowing you to easily evaluate your progress.

In most cases the Life Principle involved will dictate the nature of the action steps you will want to take. For example, if the goal is to have a positive self-image, you need specific goals that will allow or help that to happen. You might have goals relative to:

- Relationships.
- Self-care or self-live activities.
- Attitudes.
- Stress.

Think about specific situations that will likely arise for you where it would be easy to allow a negative self-image to cause you not to perform well or not believe in yourself.

If your primary self-image problem is body-image and appearance, then only develop action steps for that subject. When you develop your action steps relative to your body-image, focus on the areas that cause you difficulty. Don't bother with areas where you don't really have any serious issues.

ACTION STEPS – FIRST DRAFT

Following is a list of subjects for developing your action steps. You can do all of them or just those that you expect will produce the results you want. Your ultimate objective is to end up with 4 to 6 action steps you intend to implement in your life. You will have other actions (maybe a large number) on your initial list, but the ultimate goal is 4 to 6 good steps that you are confident will have a significant impact on achieving your objectives.

IMPORTANT: Produce as many good ideas as possible in this listing process. They may be useful at a later date.

ACTION STEPS – Initial List

INSTRUCTION: Do each of the following in order to produce an initial list of actions steps for making the Identity Life Principle a reality in your life. After you produce this initial list you will consolidate and remove the ideas that are not on target. We suggest doing this initial list in a separate notebook or on your tablet or computer.

Step #1 – TIPS FOR IMPROVEMENT

You have actually done much of the work for utilizing the tips we have discussed. In chapters 3 through 12 we provided tips on how you might improve a particular character trait. You were asked to highlight 1 to 3 suggestions you thought might work best for you and to list any other ideas you had that would improve that trait.

Go back through the entire list of tips you chose and the ideas you added and select the ones you might actually want to use as action steps. Select the ones that would have the most positive impact on the Identity Life Principle. Choose the best 4 to 12 tips, and write them in the space below in any order. [The tips are located on pages 27, 94, 101, 110, 114, 122, 131, and 138].

TIPS:

1.

_____

2.

_____

3.

_____

4.

_____

5.

_____

6.

_____

7.

_____

8.

_____

9.

_____

10.

_____

11.

_____

12.

_____

CHOOSE THE BEST TIPS:

From the list above, choose the top 4 to 6 tips and list them in <u>priority</u> order:

1.

_____

2.

_____

3.

_____

4.

_____

5.

_____

6.

_____

Make one or more of these tips the first entries on your to your master list of Initial Action Steps.

Step #2 – IMPLEMENTATION TECHNIQUES

It will be helpful for you to think about implementation techniques before you begin determining your final action steps. These are techniques you can utilize to help you achieve your goals. You might automatically mentally use some of these concepts when you are developing and working your plan. But if they are not already second nature to you, they could be part of your action steps.

Be Intentional. If you are going to accomplish anything of value, change some part of your life, or achieve a goal, you will need both discipline and intentionality. Developing a plan and even writing down action steps will accomplish very little unless you actually follow through. You must be committed, disciplined, and intentional.

Be open to change. Change is occurring daily all around us. If we are rigid and not open to new ways and new ideas, it is often difficult to accept good advice. For example, how can new ways to communicate help your self-image?

Seek knowledge and understanding. We cannot afford to be ignorant. Those with skills and expertise can teach us much. Seek new understandings rather than remain in a rut because "that's the way it has always been done."

Seek help. Ask trusted friends for advice or assistance.

Have an accountability partner. Find someone to hold you accountable for the commitments and actions steps of your Plan.

Recruit a fellow participant. Find someone who is also interested in making changes in their life and travel the path together. Not only can they support you, but you can help them succeed. Your paths do not need to be the same: the purpose is encouragement, not counsel.

Maximize use of your strengths. If you are making significant changes in your life, utilize your strengths to assist in your success. You are likely to be more successful if you use your existing strengths than your weaknesses.

Make good decisions. Much of our success in life occurs when we make right, good, and proper choices. If this has been difficult for you in the past, make this one of your action steps.

Apply filters. Filter out of your life people, places, and situations that create temptations that would hinder your goal to achieve the Identity Life Principle. For example, if you are fighting an alcohol addiction, you should not spend time in bars. If you are having trouble with honesty and integrity, you can't associate with people who lie and are untrustworthy.

Review the "IMPLEMENTATION TECHNIQUES" above and determine which techniques might be effective for your purposes. Include those techniques as action steps on your initial list.

Step #3 – CHARACTER ISSUES

Look back over Chapters 13 and 14 and identify situations that will make your commitment to the Identity Life Principle difficult to achieve. Also, think about actions that would make the Life Principle easier to achieve if they existed or were true. Then write out action steps that would advance your ability to achieve confidence and a positive self-image in your life.

1. What personal characteristics in the "Life Analysis – Know Yourself" section need to be

modified in order to achieve the Identity Life Principle?

2. Think about the times or situations when you have a low or negative self-image. Develop initial action steps that would prevent those situations from occurring or at least be under your control in the future.

Step #4 – LIFE VALUES

What Life Values (core values, priorities and commitments) require action steps in order to achieve the Identity Life Principle? Add them to your list.

Step #5 – WHAT IF I FAIL?

Do you need any action steps relative to what you will do if something fails? Think in advance what you will do if you have a temporary lapse or failure of some kind. For example, if your goal is a positive body-image what will you do if you get stressed out over your appearance? One possible action step might be to reduce your time on social media if that is a source of stress, engage in specific self-talk and the same time every day, or meditate and pray about it for five minutes every day.

If you don't add an action step for possible failures, at a minimum you should think about the possible situations that might occur and know what you are going to do if they occur.

Step #6 – BRAIN STORMING

If you aren't satisfied with your list, try to think of other options. If you can't do that on your own, get a few friends to help you brainstorm the topics on which you need more input. The purpose here is to accumulate ideas, not evaluate them. You will do the evaluating later. Seek any kind of ideas! Often one seemingly crazy idea leads to a very good one.

Step #7 – CULL AND CONSOLIDATE

You should have a substantial list of steps and ideas after doing all of the above. Now it's time to finalize your initial list.

1. Reduce the list to the <u>good</u> and <u>workable</u> ideas. Remove anything you do not want to keep on your list.

2. Eliminate or combine the duplicates into similar groupings or headings.

3. Consolidate the similar ideas into one. You may want to have sub-points for the larger ideas.

4. Prioritize the groups and sub-groups.

5. Save this list permanently.

EXAMPLES

Your list might include statements like:

a. I will have a daily quiet time that focuses on the positive aspects of my life.

b. I will journal each day about the positive things in my life.

c. If I make a mistake or fall into bad habits I will forgive myself and fix the problem immediately.

d. Every month for the next six months I will undertake a new and different hobby or pursuit that fits my strengths and skills.

e. I will stop dieting and undertake a new and permanent eating plan – a new health lifestyle.

f. I will stop worrying about things I cannot control and focus my energy on things I can control.

LIFE PLANNING ADVICE

GENERAL

Depending on your circumstances, seeking to improve your self-image could be challenging and require taking responsibility on your part. If your self-image or body-image is poor, it is probably going to take some time to build up trust in yourself. Patience and perseverance must be your watch-words during this period of time.

You will need to be decisive and make good decisions that will assist in making progress. Be steadfast. Don't allow the first setback to detour you from the goal.

Finally take responsibility! This is your life and if you want it to improve and if you want to overcome negative thinking or tendencies in your life, you will have to make it happen. Friends may be willing to help, but the responsibility is on your shoulders to achieve a positive self-image.

KEY TO SUCCESS

We believe that a key attribute for success is being committed to the goal. If you are not really committed, it won't matter how much focus or courage you exhibit, you will quit or slow to a crawl.

Make it a personal challenge that you will remain steadfast, no matter what happens. No matter what people may think or say, remain committed to the goal of a positive self-image. Become comfortable and confident in who you are. The reward is great.

FINAL ACTION STEPS

SUBJECT: **POSITIVE SELF-IMAGE**

GOAL: *To be confident in who I am.*

FINAL ACTION STEPS:
Choose the 4 to 6 best action steps from your initial list and enter them below

1.

_____

_____

_____

2.

_____

_____

_____

3.

_____

_____

_____

4.

_____

_____

_____

5.

_____

_____

_____

6.

_____

_____

_____

TECHNOLOGY: Consider entering information or reminders on your phone, tablet, or computer.

REVIEW

Before you finalize your Action Steps, you should step back and take a broader look at what you have prepared.

1. CORE VALUES & PRIORITIES: Are your action steps consistent with your core values and revised life priorities?

_____

_____

_____

2. FAMILY: Are your action steps consistent with your family's expectations?

_____

_____

_____

> a. Do you need to tell any of your family members about your plans?
> b. Do you want to ask a family member for help?
> c. Will anything you do in this plan impact a family member? If so, you may need to talk with them before you start.

3. PERSONAL COMMITMENT: Are your action steps consistent with your personal desires and commitments? Are you ready to make these changes in your life? Are you missing anything important?

_____

_____

_____

Go back and modify your plans, if necessary.

GETTING STARTED

If you are excited and ready to begin, go for it! Begin with any or all of the above action steps.

But if you have any fear or reluctance, start slowly. There is absolutely no reason to try to do everything at once. Choose the action step that you think will be the easiest to achieve and get started. When that is implemented, choose the next easiest action step, and proceed through the list in that manner.

Some people may have a preference to do the most difficult one first and get that out of the way. That's fine if that works for you, but if this is going to create significant change in your life, we recommend you start slowly.

Chapter 17
Planning Part 5

Ongoing Progress Review and Evaluation

––––

IDENTITY LIFE PRINCIPLE
Be confident in who you are.

*"The life which is unexamined
is not worth living."*
Socrates[55]

FREQUENCY:

During the first eight weeks, review your plans weekly. In fact, as long as you have a significant list of action steps to accomplish you should take time weekly to evaluate your progress. At some point you can move to every two weeks and then monthly. As long as you still have things you want to implement, you should review your plan monthly.

We recommend you put this review time on your calendar and allow 90 minutes for your first review and update. Based on the time needed for your first review you can schedule future reviews.

SUCCESS:

Review your plan for success and failure. What can you discontinue, what should you add, and what have you achieved? Think particularly about your goals and priorities. How are you doing? Are you making progress?

MODIFICATION:

What can be removed because it has been successfully implemented? What is not working? What needs to be changed? What other action steps or ideas did you set aside when you developed your initial list? Should any of these ideas be added you your plan?

Make the necessary changes and tell a friend about your successes!

Check List

If you like to use check lists in completing tasks we have included a check list in Appendix B that lists all the steps in completing your Plan.

Chapter 18

Hope & Encouragement

What you place your hope in
will define the path for your life.

General

In "*Animal Dreams*" Barbara Kingsolver writes, *"The very least you can do in your life is figure out what you hope for. And the most you can do is live inside that hope. Not admire it from a distance but live right in it, under its roof."*[66]

Hope is a very important component of our existence. You may not always be conscious of your hope, but it's what drives you forward; it is the inherent desire of your heart. It is often masked by other mental or emotional baggage, but it is there nevertheless.

Kingsolver's point is that we need to unmask that hope, embrace it, and intentionally bring it into our lives. We must not just think about it or admire it, but make it a part of our lives. Why? Because what we hope for will define the course of our lives. It defines what is ultimately important to us and it will shape our priorities.

What do you hope for?

MERRIAM-WEBSTER's definition of hope is to desire, with the expectation of obtaining the object of that desire. Genuine hope is not wishful thinking, but a firm assurance about things that are "unseen" and still in the future.

Hope looks ahead to a future expectation that is uplifting or optimistic. The opposite of hope is depression, sadness, or dejection. We can have different hopes for the many parts of our lives. Some are little hopes and others are large. Some may be huge. Lives can be built and lost on the nature of our hope.

What are your hopes? Take a few minutes before you proceed to think about and identify some of your hopes. What do you hope for? What hope sustains you? Are you conscious of your hopes? What hope would sustain you if you were living in dire circumstances? Jot down some notes about your thoughts on "hope:"

_____

_____

_____

_____

_____

_____

_____

"Loyalty is what makes us trust.
Trust is what makes us stay.
Staying is what makes us love,
and love is what gives us hope."
Glenn van Dekken[67]

The Result of Hope

Many wise sayings about hope indicate that righteous people hope for joy or happiness but the destiny of wicked people is misery. What does it mean that the righteous hope for joy? Why joy? What is joy? Someone with joy has an inner peace, they are at rest, and they have a feeling of well-being. Typically joyful people are confident, assured, and have frequent feelings of happiness. If you ask them what or how they are feeling, they will often respond, "*Great!*"

Hope placed in evil and wickedness will not end well. Trouble is on the horizon, if it has not already arrived. Problems and suffering are the typical results for making bad choices, usually the result of bad information, bad advice, or poor thinking.

Such trouble and suffering means loss, depression, mental anguish, lack of energy, and general despair. People often describe this feeling as "heartache." It can be said that this produces a broken spirit which can be debilitating because one feels lost, that no one cares, and life does not seem worthwhile. The meaning of life has been lost.

What meaning does life have for you?

*"They say a person needs just three things
to be truly happy in this world:
someone to love, something to do,
and something to hope for."*
Tom Bodett[68]

Three Psychiatrists

In the period leading up to WW2 there were three Jewish psychiatrists: two learned masters in the field, and one young apprentice. The first master was a man named Sigmund Freud. He had spent years studying people, striving to understand what made people tick. He had reached the conclusion that the most basic drive in the human being was the drive for pleasure. He concluded that it is our need for pleasure that explains why we do what we do, how we live.

The second master was Alfred Adler. He too spent years studying human behavior. His studies led him to disagree with Sigmund Freud. Adler was convinced that the explanation for human behavior was power. All of us grow up feeling inferior and powerless. He concluded that life was a drive to gain control, to feel we are important.

The third man was a young up-and-coming psychiatrist by the name of Victor Frankl. He hoped to follow in the footsteps of his mentors. But before his career gained any momentum WW2 started. The Nazis invaded and life became dangerous for Jews. Freud and Adler were world renowned scholars and managed to escape before Hitler invaded. Frankl was not so lucky. He was arrested and thrown into a Nazi concentration camp for four long years.

After the war was over, Frankl was released from the concentration camp and resumed his career. As he reflected upon his time as a prisoner, he realized something quite strange: the people who survived were not always the ones you'd expect. Many who were physically strong wasted away and died. Others who were seemingly physically weak survived. Why? What was it that enabled them to hang on through a living hell?

Frankl reflected on the theories of his mentors. Freud's pleasure principle couldn't explain it. For desperate and terrible years the people in that camp knew only pain, suffering and degradation. Pleasure was not a word in their vocabulary. It wasn't pleasure that kept them going.

What then of Adler's theory about power being the basic human need? That didn't hold up well either. Frankl and his fellow Jews were completely powerless during their time in the concentration camps. Each day they stared down the barrels of loaded guns, were treated like animals, and suffered jackboots on their faces. They had no power and no prospect of power.

Victor Frankl came up with his own theory. The difference between those who survived and those who perished was *hope*. Those who survived never gave up their belief that their lives had meaning, that despite everything going on around them, this period would one day end and they would again live meaningful and purposeful lives.[69]

The one thing that gives life value, that gives us purpose, is that we live with a sense of hope and that our life has meaning. If there is no meaning in life, then why bother? Life reverts to chaos where there is no purpose and hope – no meaning. Do I exist to give myself pleasure and then disappear into the mist without meaning? Does that make any sense to you? There are people who believe that nonsense. I don't. I firmly believe that I exist because life does have meaning.

"Once you choose hope,
anything's possible."
Christopher Reeve[70]

The Time is Now

Life goes by quickly. Elderly people looking back at their youth are particularly and poignantly aware of the passing years. The prime of life is fleeting. Thus, it is wise not to put off until tomorrow what you can do today. The time is *now*. If you do it now you won't forget about it, and won't have to worry about getting it done before some deadline. You may even be able to enjoy the fruit of your labor.

This is good advice for everyone, but particularly important for those in the prime of life. We certainly have enough freedom in life to do most of the things we want and we should and can enjoy life. Although we are often told to follow our hearts, we also need to use wisdom in making good choices.

What is Your Hope?

List the most significant "hopes" in your life? Quiet your spirit and take time to really think about what you truly hope for. What are your life hopes? What are the deep desires of your heart?

_____

_____

_____

_____

_____

_____

_____

Following are some possibilities:

1. that I am right with my God.
2. that I am a faithful and loving spouse or parent.
3. that I am a faithful and true leader in my family.
4. that I am a valued friend.
5. that my children have genuine joy in life.
6. that I use my skills, gifts, and resources wisely.
7. that I am honest and true, never misleading anyone.
8. that I serve my community well.
9. that my children marry spouses who truly love them.
10. that I impact and improve someone's life.
11. that I have a life of good health.
12. that my extended family truly love one another.
13. that I will marry the love of my life.
14. that I will live to spoil my grandbabies.
15. that I will live to see my grandchildren marry.

Now go back to your list and identify the top five and prioritize them. How do your hopes fit with your Life Plan? Are they in harmony with your plans?

"Hope itself is like a star — not to be seen
in the sunshine of prosperity, and only
to be discovered in the night of adversity."
Charles H. Spurgeon[71]

Don't Hope in Wealth

If one or more of your hopes is in money or wealth, erase it, or cross it out. Destroy it! Hope placed in wealth fails. It is fleeting. It is fickle and it will not last. Hope in wealth comes from worldly values that disappear and can be lost forever at any time. The problem is we can tend to fall in

194

love with money and the power it brings. Loving luxury, power, and wealth is at the root of so much trouble.

The Source of Hope

Many proverbs and wise sayings identify the source of hope as "wisdom." Wisdom is permanent. It is extremely valuable because it can guide your decisions in life. Wisdom can give us a future so we have something to look forward to (to hope in). It will not fade away like a mist after a storm. It will not vanish in the face of trouble.

Wisdom will guide us in making right decisions.

ATTITUDES AND ACTIONS THAT ENCOURAGE HOPE

- Be patient!
- Share your difficulties with a trusted friend.
- Don't be constantly critical of life.
- Focus on what's important. Give little time to the little things.
- Understand that life has challenges. Everyone experiences tough times. You are not alone in that.
- Don't live in fear. Learn and grow from difficult times. Seek understanding from life situations.
- Be kind to yourself. Celebrate victories.
- Life is a journey, not a party.
- Be content with what you have.
- Be intentional: choose hope instead of fear.

TIPS FOR BEING HOPEFUL:

- Look on the bright side. Be an optimist, not a pessimist. Be positive and encourage others.
- Have an attitude of gratitude. Be a thankful person.
- See the humor in the human condition. Laugh at yourself. Don't take life too seriously.
- Listen to <u>good</u> music, read <u>good</u> books, watch <u>good</u> movies, and have <u>good</u> friends . . . (GIGO).
- Be healthy: take care of yourself physically (sleep, food, drink, and exercise).
- Avoid bad habits: alcohol, drugs, immorality, etc.
- Live and work in positive surroundings. Minimize exposure to negative influences.
- Have a life plan. Set goals. Know where you are going. Have a sense of purpose.
- Be organized. Have a to-do list and a schedule.

"Hope is medicine for a
soul that's sick and tired."
Eric Swensson[72]

Chapter 19
Implementation Techniques

FREE BONUS CHAPTER

At this point you have completed your plan, including 4 to 6 action steps and you are ready to begin. But you may need a little more encouragement in getting started.

If you would like a free bonus chapter (PDF) that provides additional help on subjects like:

- Self-discipline
- Intentionality
- Choosing filters
    Filter what you see
    Filter what you hear
    Filter where you go
    Filter what you say
- Accountability partner

Go to: www.lifeplanningtools.link/techniques

Appendix A – How to Prioritize

General

What are your objectives? What's most important considering your responsibilities, plans, and goals? You will need to be relentless in sticking to your priorities. Like your life and career, your priorities change over time.

General questions to think about and guide the process of setting priorities:

- What needs to be done *now*?
- What is most important?
- What happens if it doesn't get done?
- When do you need to begin?
- What materials, resources and skills do you need to accomplish the objective?

The Process

1. MAKE A LIST
Write a list of all your tasks. Identify any due dates for time-sensitive tasks. It is important to maintain an up-to-date list and also wise to keep an electronic back-up of the master list. Your master "to-do" list serves as a running log of what you want to accomplish over time.

2. ASSIGN STATUS / TIME FRAME
Assign a time frame. For example, this task needs to be accomplished today, this week, this month, this quarter, or this year. Identify the date you want to begin.

3. URGENCY/IMPORTANCE/PRIORITY

Identify the urgent versus the important tasks. Ignore anything else unless your list is <u>very</u> short. Choose one of the following methods:

a. Scale Method: On a scale of 1 to 10 (or 1 to 100) assess value or importance.

b. Other Simple Strategies

- Do the most important task first.
- Do the most impactful task first.
- Complete one major task at a time.
- Do a simple high/medium/low assignment.

4. FLEXIBILITY

Be flexible. Situations and circumstances can change very quickly. Re-evaluate your priority list frequently. If priorities change, move on to the next priority. Know when to stop working on a goal or action step. Make sure that what you are doing warrants your time.

Appendix B – Check List

If you like to use check lists in completing tasks, we have included a check list that lists all the steps in completing the Plan.

Chapter 13: Planning Part 1 – Life Analysis, Know Yourself

☐ List the things and activities you love to do.

☐ List your greatest physical or mental skills and abilities.

☐ List your strengths, special skills, and serious passions.

☐ List your weaknesses.

☐ List any roadblocks, distractions, or hindrances that might prevent you from implementing the Identity Life Principle.

☐ List any serious character flaws.

Chapter 14: Planning Part 2 – Life Values

☐ List your final 5 to 8 Core Values.

☐ List your top 6 to 12 Life Priorities today.

☐ How would your Life Priorities change if you knew you had only two years to live?

☐ How would the Identity Life Principle or any new objectives change your current Life Priorities?

☐ How should the Life Analysis in Chapter 13 change your Priorities?

☐ Given the Identity Life Principle, what new priorities would you need to adopt?

☐ Prepare a final list of your revised Life Priorities. Aim at 6 to 8, but no more than 12.

☐ List the existing traits, behaviors, activities, or habits you must manage in order to achieve the Identity Life Principle.

☐ List your final 4 to 8 Life Commitments.

Chapter 15: Planning Part 3 – Identity Life Principle

The Life Goal is: *I will be confident in who I am.*

IDENTITY LIFE PRINCIPLE: Be confident in who you are.

Chapter 16: Planning Part 4 – Action Steps

☐ Select and list of the best 4 to 10 tips. The tips are located on pages 27, 94, 101, 110, 114, 122, 131, and 138.

☐ Choose the top 4 to 6 tips and list them in priority order.

☐ Choose and list the implementation techniques that would be helpful to you in implementing your plan.

☐ Produce and list your initial list of actions steps for making the Identity Life Principle a reality in your life.

☐ Cull and consolidate the initial list.

☐ List action steps for those situations that will make your commitment to the Identity Life Principle difficult to achieve.

☐ List the existing personal characteristics that must be improved to achieve your objectives.

☐ List the core values, priorities, or commitments that require action steps in order to achieve the Identity Life Principle.

☐ List the 2 to 6 "Tips For Improvement" that you feel would be particularly effective for you.

☐ Reduce the working list to only the good and workable ideas. Eliminate or combine the duplicates.

☐ Identify and list the helpful "TECHNIQUES FOR IMPLEMENTATION" that warrant inclusion in your action steps.

☐ List action steps relative to what you will do if something fails.

☐ Cull and consolidate the list.

☐ Prioritize the groups and the individual actions within groups.

☐ FINAL ACTION STEPS: Choose the 4 to 6 best action steps from your list.

☐ TECHNOLOGY: Consider entering information or reminders on your phone, tablet, or computer.

☐ REVIEW:
   a) Are your action steps consistent with your core values and revised life priorities?
   b) Are your action steps consistent with your family's expectations? Do you need to communicate with your family?
   c) Are your action steps consistent with your personal desires and commitments?

☐ Modify your plans as necessary.

Chapter 17: Planning Part 5 – Ongoing Progress Review

☐ During the first eight weeks, review your plans weekly.

☐ Review your plan for success and failure. Make necessary changes.

☐ Modify and update your plan as needed.

"To be yourself in a world that is constantly trying to make you something else is the greatest accomplishment."

Ralph Waldo Emerson[73]

"Don't compromise yourself. You are all you've got."

Janis Joplin[74]

Transformation Roadmap
Wisdom That Transforms!

1. Your identity is rooted in inner values. Living your best life begins with building a strong foundation of core values, moral standards, and purpose. These internal qualities define your identity and provide stability.

2. A positive self-image is essential in life. By seeking areas of growth and actively working to redefine how you view yourself, you can overcome many challenges.

3. Living your best life requires actively selecting relationships, values, habits, and influences that align with your life purpose. You hold the power to define your self-image through deliberate actions, such as choosing mentors, prioritizing health, and cultivating core values.

4. True fulfillment comes from grounding your identity in internal values rather than external validations like wealth, societal norms, or others' opinions.

5. Recognize that your identity is a journey of change and progress, especially during times of stress or transition.

6. Avoid basing your self-image on external factors like appearance, accomplishments, or other people's opinions. Value your unique qualities and abilities by being comfortable with yourself.

7. Resist conforming to external pressures from society, social media, or others' expectations, and instead cultivate self-awareness and embrace your unique values, beliefs, and passions.

8. Recognize and address the signs of a distorted self-image, such as low self-esteem, constant self-criticism, or reliance on external validation. Actively challenge negative thought patterns and focus on your strengths and values.

9. Recognize that life is a series of seasons, each with unique challenges and opportunities. Difficult times are temporary and positive seasons should be fully appreciated. Maintain a balanced perspective.

10. Dismiss false narratives concerning appearance, abilities, accomplishments, possessions, and other people's opinions. Instead base your self-image on an internal sense of value.

11. Recognize that many body-image issues stem from unrealistic societal standards perpetuated by social media and advertising. You can actively challenge these false narratives by prioritizing your health and well-being.

12. Replace negative self-talk with a positive internal dialogue and reduce exposure to harmful social media.

13. Embrace being yourself and resist the urge to compare yourself to others, especially on social media, as manipulated data can distort your perception of reality.

14. Allow yourself to be vulnerable and accept help from others. Surround yourself with positive people who respect and support you.

Your decisions shape your life. Start building with intention!

Your Next Steps

Change Your Life with purpose and intention!

Should you read other books in this series?

We recommend that if you acquire any books in the Series, you should also obtain *CHOOSE Integrity*. This is the foundational book in the series. We also believe the four books covering the other Primary Life Principles would be particularly useful for living a better life: Friends, Speech, Diligence (Work), and Money.

CHOOSE Faith

This is a unique book in the Series. It addresses all the important spiritual type questions you might consider. It answers questions like: Does God exist? Why should I care about faith? What's religion all about? Does eternal life really exist? I don't know the right questions to ask. What is the truth? This book will help you find answers to your spiritual questions.

LIFE PLANNING HANDBOOK

This book is also unique. If you are interested in doing a complete life plan that covers all aspects of your life, not just a specific topic like those addressed in The Life Planning Series, go to:

https://www.amazon.com/dp/1952359325

You can live a better life.
Just Decide You Want to!

The Life Planning Series

These books can improve your life.

LIFE PLANNING HANDBOOK	**A Life Plan will shape your life journey!** The next step in your life planning.
CHOOSE INTEGRITY	**Life Principle:** Be honest, live with integrity, and base your life on truth.
CHOOSE FRIENDS WISELY	**Life Principle:** Choose your friends wisely.
CHOOSE THE RIGHT WORDS	**Life Principle:** Guard your speech.
CHOOSE GOOD WORK HABITS	**Life Principle:** Be diligent and a hard worker.
CHOOSE FINANCIAL RESPONSIBILITY	**Life Principle:** Make sound financial choices.

CHOOSE A POSITIVE SELF-IMAGE	**Life Principle:** Be confident in who you are.
CHOOSE LEADERSHIP	**Life Principle:** Lead well and be a loyal follower.
CHOOSE CORE VALUES	**Life Principle:** Core values will drive your life.
CHOOSE LOVE AND FAMILY	**Life Principle:** Build strong relationships.
CHOOSE FAITH	*Your Spiritual Guidebook for Questions about Religion, God, Heaven, Truth, Evil, and the Afterlife.*

Go to: **https://www.amazon.com/dp/B09TH9SYC4**
to get your copy.

Create a life based on purpose, meaning, and lasting fulfillment.

Acknowledgments

My wife has patiently persevered while I indulged my interest in this subject. Thank you for your patience.

Our older daughter has been an invaluable resource. She has also graciously produced our website at www.lifeplanningtools.com

Our middle daughter designed all the covers for this series. We are very grateful for her help, talent and creativity.

Notes

QUOTES

ACCURACY: We have used a number of quotes throughout this book that came from our files, notes, books, public articles, the Internet, etc. We have made no attempt to verify that these quotes were actually written or spoken by the person they are attributed to. Regardless of the source of these quotes, the wisdom of the underlying message is relative to the content in this book and worth noting, even if the source reference is erroneous.

SOURCE: Unless otherwise specifically noted below the quotes used herein can be sourced from a number of different websites on the Internet that provide lists of quotes by subject or author. The same or similar quotes will appear on multiple sites. Therefore, rather than assign individual quote sources, we are providing a list of sites where we might have found the quotes that were used in this book:

--azquotes.com
--brainyquote.com
--codeofliving.com
--everydaypower.com
--goodhousekeeping.com
--goodreads.com/quotes
--graciousquotes.com
--inc.com
--keepinspiring.me
--notable-quotes.com
--parade.com
--plantetofsuccess.com
--quotemaster.org
--quotir.com
--success.com
--thoughtco.com
--thoughtcatalog.com
--wisdomquotes.com
--wisesayings.com
--wow4u.com

1 Brigham Young, see QUOTES above.
2 Stephen H Berkey, www.amazon.com/author/stephenhberkey
3 Latin American saying, see QUOTES above.
4 Aesop, see QUOTES above.
5 SermonCentral.com, contributed by Perry Greene.
6 --

7 --

8 A large number of Internet sites. Search for "Jonathan Edwards," "Max Jukes," or "A. E. Winship."

9 Roger Crawford, see QUOTES above.

10 Cicero, see QUOTES above.

11 Joyce Brothers, see QUOTES above.

12 Eleanor Roosevelt, see QUOTES above.

13 Maxwell Maltz, see QUOTES above.

14 Anthony Trollope, see QUOTES above.

15 Roy Baumeister Ph. D. , https://www.sciencedirect.com/science/article/pii/B9780121346454500275

16 Guy Finley, see QUOTES above.

17 Gabriel García Márquez, see QUOTES above.

18 Yvonne I Wilson, see QUOTES above.

19 Oscar Wilde, see QUOTES above.

20 A study on The World Counts website: https://www.theworldcounts.com/purpose/how-to-improve-self-image

21 Dietrich Bonhoeffer, see QUOTES above.

22 Ralph Waldo Emerson, see QUOTES above.

23 Mark Twain, see QUOTES above.

24 Nadège Richards, see QUOTES above.

25 Henry David Thoreau, see QUOTES above.

26 Ayn Rand, see QUOTES above.

27 Lore Ferguson, Christianity Today, *Beautiful Beyond Our Control,* October 27, 2014.

28 Stacey London, see QUOTES above.

29 Bible, Solomon, Ecclesiastes 2:1.

30 Andre Gide, see QUOTES above.

31 Dr. Roopleen, see QUOTES above.

32 Norman Vincent Peale, see QUOTES above.

33 Becca Lee, see QUOTES above.

34 Nido R Qubein, see QUOTES above.

35 Madonna, see QUOTES above.

36 Lilly Harry, see QUOTES above.

37 Sarah Dessen, see QUOTES above.

38 Steve Maraboli, see QUOTES above.

39 Buddha, see QUOTES above.

40 Norman Vincent Peale, see QUOTES above.

41 Mae West, see QUOTES above.

42 Louise Hay, see QUOTES above.

43 Denis Waitley, see QUOTES above.

44 Nathaniel Branden, see QUOTES above.

45 Benjamin Spock, see QUOTES above.

46 Shannon L. Alder, see QUOTES above.

47 Thaddeus Golas, see QUOTES above.

48 Malcolm S. Forbes, see QUOTES above.

49 Deepak Chopra, see QUOTES above.

50 Dennis Lehane, see QUOTES above.

51 Marie Curie , see QUOTES above.
52 Kenneth Blanchard, see QUOTES above.
53 Les Brown, see QUOTES above.
54 Brian Tracy, see QUOTES above.
55 Socrates, see QUOTES above.
56 Amelia Earhart, see QUOTES above.
57 Bob Proctor, see QUOTES above.
58-65 -none-
66 Barbara Kingsolver. *Animal Dreams*, Harper Perennial; Reissue edition (2013), ISBN-13: 978-0062278500.
67 Glenn van Dekken, see QUOTES above.
68 Tom Bodett, see QUOTES above.
69 Victor Frankl, Based on a talk given by Australian speaker Michael Frost.
70 Christopher Reeve, see QUOTES above.
71 Charles H. Spurgeon, see QUOTES above.
72 Eric Swensson, see QUOTES above.
73 Ralph Waldo Emerson, see QUOTES above.
74 Janis Joplin, see QUOTES above.

General References

1. How to Overcome Your Self-Image Issues and Build a Positive Self-Image, Self Care, By Himani, https://therapymantra.co/self-care/self-image-issues.
2. Self Image Issues: Signs, Effects, Causes, Solution, Self Care, Therapy, by Reena Singh, https://mantracare.org/therapy.
3. *Self Esteem*, 20 June, 2022, What is Self-Image and How Do We Improve it? Definition + Quotes, 22 Dec 2018 by Courtney E. Ackerman, https://positivepsychology.com/category/the-self.
4. Positive Thinking - 4 Signs You Have a Distorted Self-Image (And How To Fix It), Fabio De Sio, https://www.lifehack.org/author/fabiodesio.
5. Body Image Issues: How to Improve Negative Self-Image, Medically reviewed by Marney A. White, PhD, MS, Psychology — Written by Rory Stobo on April 29, 2022, https://greatist.com/connect/stop-being-disappointed-with-your-body,
6. Self-Esteem, 4 Ways to Determine If You Have Self-Esteem Issues, Posted September 16, 2016, https://www.psychologytoday.com/us/basics/self-esteem.
7. Seven Ways to Overcome Negative Self-Image, Amanda, Jan 9, 2020, https://www.gr8ness.com/seven-ways-to-overcome-negative-self-image.
8. Troubled Teens and Self-Identity: Causes, Problems, and Common Behaviors, April 4, 2018,by Josh Watson, LCSW, https://aspiroadventure.com/blog/troubled-teens-and-self-identity-causes-problems-and-common-behaviors.
9. Risky Behavior in Teens: What Parents Should Know, October 25 2021, by Shannon Weaver, https://aspiroadventure.com/blog/risky-behavior.

10. Identity Issues, https://www.goodtherapy.org/blog/psychpedia.
11. Help! Who Am I? 7 Signs That You Suffer From an Identity Crisis, Last reviewed by Sheri Jacobson May 8, 2014, https://thecoachspace.com/blog/signs-that-you-are-going-through-an-identity-crisis/
12. Irina Berdzenishvili, Personal Identity 101: Identity Problems: Am I Good Enough? https://www.byarcadia.org/post/personal-identity-101-identity-problems-am-i-good-enough.
13. Identity Problems: Am I Good Enough? *"Who am I? They mock me, these lonely questions of mine."* (Dietrich Bonhoeffer, 1945)
14. What is Self-Identity? Author: Reed Hepler, Expert Contributor; Jennifer Levitas, Explore what self-identity is and why it's important. Learn the components of self-identity theory, ways people shape their self-identity, and how it can change. Updated: 02/15/2022, https://study.com/learn/lesson/self-identity-theory-examples.html#section---SelfIdentityExamples
15. What Is an Identity Crisis? By Kendra Cherry, Updated on February 17, 2022, Medically reviewed by Daniel B. Block, MD, mantracare.org/therapy/issues/identity-crisis/
16. What is Self-Love and Why Is It So Important? Why Is Self-Love So Important? (30 Experts Share Their Best Advice), By Martin Caparrotta, Updated on 24 October 2020, https://humanwindow.com/why-is-self-love-important.
17. Self-Love: Definition, Tips, Examples, and Exercises, By Tchiki Davis, MA, PhD, https://www.berkeleywellbeing.com/self-love.html.
18. 8 Powerful Steps to Self-Love, Posted June 29, 2017, Reviewed by Devon Frye, https://www.psychologytoday.com/us/blog/the-mindful-self-express/201706/8-powerful-steps-self-love.
19. 34 Ways to Practice Self-Love and Be Good to Yourself, Last Updated on July 4, 2022, Jade Nyx, https://www.lifehack.org/.../30-ways-practice-self-love-and-good-yourself.html.
20. How to Love Yourself For Real, According to Therapists, By Amanda McCracken, https://www.self.com/story/how-to-love-yourself.
21. ELEVEN SELF LOVE ACTIVITIES (THAT CAN CHANGE YOUR LIFE), by Chloe Parpworth-Reynolds, https://subconsciousservant.com/self-love-activities, Jun 05, 2020.
22. How to Love Yourself Using These 20 Self-Love Tips, by Katherine Hurst, https://thelawofattraction.com/love-yourself.
23. Self-Worth: 4 Ways to Improve Your Self Esteem, By Tchiki Davis, MA, PhD, https://www.berkeleywellbeing.com/recover-your-self-worth.html.

About the Author

The author graduated from the Business School at Indiana University and obtained a master's degree at Georgia State University in Atlanta. His first career was as a senior executive with a top insurance and financial institution, where he spent a number of years directing strategic planning for one of their major divisions.

In the 1990s he founded an online Internet business which he sold in 2010. He began to write and publish books and materials that led to an interest in personal life planning. This resulted in combining the wisdom of wise sayings and proverbs with life planning and the result is the Life Planning Series and the Life Planning Handbook.

The author, his wife, and two of his children and their families live in the Nashville, TN area.

WEBSITE: http://www.lifeplanningtools.com

AMAZON: www.amazon.com/author/jswellman

Contact Us

	www.lifeplanningtools.com info@lifeplanningtools.com	Website Email
Facebook	JSWellman	
	www.amazon.com/author/jswellman	**Author Page**
Life Planning Series	www.amazon.com/dp/B09TH9SYC4	
	www.lifeplanningtools.link/newsletter	**Monthly News Letter**

You can help

IDEAS and SUGGESTIONS: If you have a suggestion to improve this book, please let us know.

Mention our LIFE PLANNING books on your social platforms and recommend them to your family and friends.

Thank you!

Make a Difference

"The law of prosperity is generosity.
If you want more, give more."
Bob Proctor[57]

Have you ever done something just out of kindness or goodwill without wanting or expecting anything in return? I'm going to ask you to do <u>two things</u> just for that reason. The first will be just out of the goodness of your heart and the second to make an impact in someone else's life.

It won't cost you anything and it won't take a lot of time or effort.

This Book

First, what did you think of this book? Give the book an honest review in order for us to compete with the giant publishers. What did you like and how did it impact you? It will only take you several minutes to leave your review at:
https://www.amazon.com/dp/1952359430

Follow the link above to the Amazon sales page, scroll down about three quarters of the page and click the box that says: "Write a customer review." It does not have to be long or well-written – just tell other readers what you think about the book. Or, just score the book on a scale of 1 – 5 stars (5 is high).

This will help us a great deal and we so appreciate your willingness to help. If you want to tell us something about

the book directly, you can email us at:
info@lifeplanningtools.com.

Give Books to Students and Employees

Secondly, do you know any schools or organizations that might want to give this book or our Life Planning Handbook to their students or emloyees?

Here is how you can help. If you send us the contact information and allow us to use your name, we will contact the person or persons you suggest with all the details. Obviously there would be special pricing and if the order is large enough, a message from the organization's CEO could be included on the printed pages.

Alternatively, you can personally give a copy of one of our books to the organization for their consideration. We would recommend our Life Planning Handbook, but some organizations might be interested in a specific subject. If they are interested in this partnership with us, they should contact us directly.

It is not that difficult to help someone live a better life: just a little time and intentionality. Let us hear from you if you want to make a difference in someone's life!

J. S. Wellman
Extra-mile Publishing
steve@lifeplanningtools.com
www.lifeplanningtools.com

Wisdom Without Action is Just information!

IDENTITY LIFE PRINCIPLE: Be confident in who you are.

LIFE PLANNING SERIES
J.S. WELLMAN

LIFE PLANNING SERIES
J.S. WELLMAN